TED AND SUPERIOR

TED ALBERT AND THE 51st STATE OF SUPERIOR

By Bruce K. Cox

Bruce K Cox
1 June 2009

Agogeebic Press LLC

For ordering information contact:
Agogeebic Press LLC
P.O. Box 131
408A Sunday Lake Street
Wakefield, Michigan 49968

Copyright © 2009 by Bruce K. Cox

First Edition 2009

Printed by BookMasters, Inc.

ISBN: 978-0-9822390-0-1

Without limiting the rights under copyright reserved above, no part of this publication may be reproduced, stored in or introduced into a retrieval system, or transmitted, in any form, or by any means (electronic, mechanical, photocopying, recording, or otherwise) without the prior written permission of Agogeebic Press LLC, except in the case of brief quotations for the purpose of review.

ALL RIGHTS RESERVED

COVER: Picture of Ted Albert and the Upper Peninsula of Michigan. Concept by Bruce K. Cox, artwork by John DeMario.

Agogeebic Press LLC

www.gogebicbooks.com

Preface

In June of 1975 Ted Albert was vigorously pursuing his vision of turning the Upper Peninsula of Michigan into the 51st State of Superior. In the latter part of that month he announced a meeting to be held at the Community Memorial Building in Wakefield. I was then nineteen years old, and out of curiosity I attended the meeting to see what he had to say; there must have been close to a dozen people in attendance. This was my one and only acquaintance with the political maverick and dreamer who worked for years to make the U.P. into the 51st State of Superior.

The first movement for U. P. statehood began soon after Michigan was admitted to the Union in the mid-19th century, and its history is documented in the book, *Superior—A State for the North Country*, by James L. Carter. But none of the earlier movements appear to have been as serious and determined as the one led by Ted Albert in the 1970s.

One of Ted's major themes was the notion of utilizing gambling as a means of earning revenue and attracting tourists to the proposed new state. It was a bit controversial at that time, but in today's world it seems fairly mundane. Today the Upper Peninsula is dotted with Indian casinos from east to west and north to south. One can only wonder how they would have fared in a state where gambling would have been a major industry and means of funding the government.

Ted Albert led an interesting life. He was educated in the legal profession, got into politics, was elected prosecuting attorney of Gogebic County for four terms, and went back to private practice. But he never gave up politics, and was a perennial candidate for office in the county and state. His life was a continuous struggle to get elected, to clear his name with the State Bar Grievance Board, and to create the 51st State of Superior.

There is a saying, 'an unexamined life is a wasted life,' and I believe this especially applies to a dynamic person like Ted Albert. There is another old saying: 'You live as long as you are remembered.' What better reasons could one find for recording the life story of Ted Albert.

Bruce K. Cox

Ted and Superior   by Bruce K. Cox

1

THE MIDDLE EAST MEETS THE U.P.

Ted Albert possessed the tenacity of the legendary frog that clung fiercely to the huron's neck as the bird attempted to swallow it. Ted exhibited this pugnacity in his law practice, his four terms as Gogebic County Prosecuting Attorney, his political career, his battles against the State Bar Grievance Board, and his fervent promotion of separate statehood for the Upper Peninsula of Michigan as the 51st state of Superior. "The U.P.," he once said, "is a sleeping giant, used as the world's largest state park."

His father, George Albert, was born in Fih-El-Koura, in Northern Lebanon, on August 15, 1888, one of three sons of George Albert and Karem Hydar; the family's surname was originally Abdallah.[1] George Albert had brothers John, Mose and Sam, and two sisters, Mrs. George Simon and Mrs. S. Haj.

Christians inhabited the little village of Fih, located eight miles south of the city of Tripoli, up in the hills in the district of Koura. The region was known for its wine and olive oil production, and the inhabitants of its fifty-two villages were called Kouranians. The villagers raised sheep, and many species of fruit trees grew there, with olive trees and grapevines being the two most important.

---

[1] According to his marriage record he was 24 years old in 1910, which indicates 1886 as his year of birth, but the 1920 census listed his age as 31, which would appear to place his year of birth in 1888. His obituary gave August 15th as the date of his birth, while his death certificate listed August 5th. His parents' names are given as Abdallah Abdallah and Karemia Hydar on his death record, and Albert George and Carem Nickeles on his marriage record; his brother Mose's death record gives their parents' names as George Albert and Karema Hydar.

In 1865 the villagers of Fih began building a little stone church, which they completed and dedicated on September 1, 1892, the feast day of St. Simon, after whom it was named. Every year they celebrated the feast day of St. Simon, and people from surrounding towns came to join them. At the end of the 19th and beginning of the 20th century there were ten waves of emigrations from Fih to America, and George Albert and some of his siblings were among the immigrants who settled in the United States.

"Georges Abdallah" came to America aboard the *Pretoria*, a newly-built passenger ship, leaving from Beirut and thence from the port of Boulogne in France. He was accompanied by his uncle and aunt, Habib and Martha Abdallah, arriving in New York City on December 3, 1899.

George Albert's brother Samuel came to this country for a while before returning to Lebanon. His brother Mose, who was two years younger, came to America in 1907 and then returned to Lebanon before moving back to Ironwood in 1917. Mose Albert began his career as a peddler, traveling to logging camps and mining locations to peddle novelties before acquiring a shop on the southwest corner of Ayer and Suffolk. He operated a jewelry store at 131 east Ayer street, just up on the corner from the George Albert clothing store. Mose got married in later life, and remained in business until the time of his death in 1968.

The youngest brother, John Albert, immigrated in 1905 and worked as a salesman in George Albert's clothing store. Like his brother Mose, he later went into the jewelry business and had a store at 127 west Aurora, across the street from George Albert's building. John married a woman of Lebanese ancestry; he retired in 1977 and passed away in 1988 at age 95.

George Albert had "four or five years" of education back in the old country, "in Europe and Asia," an advantage he had over many other immigrants. He spoke Arabic, though he and his siblings who followed him to America all learned

English. Albert lived with his uncle and aunt in New York, then moved to Iron Mountain, Michigan for one year, then to Wilkes-Barre, Pennsylvania for a few months before returning to Iron Mountain. They were of Orthodox Christian faith, and he supported himself by selling Christian literature.

The Upper Peninsula ("U. P.") of Michigan then had a total population of about 250,000. In Iron Mountain he joined a small community of fellow Lebanese Christians, sometime later going to work as a sectionhand for the Chicago and Northwestern Railroad, traveling the rails of Upper Michigan.

Unlike the Middle East, the U.P. was a land of four seasons, with cold temperatures and heavy snowfalls during the winter months, which almost always lasted at least from December through March; the village of Fih back in Lebanon usually saw one snowfall every year. Only a couple of generations earlier the U. P. was considered by many to be nothing more than an uninviting and frozen wasteland, mostly inhabited by wolves and mosquitoes.

Iron Mountain, located in the south central U. P., was an iron ore mining town with a flourishing little business district located mainly along Stephenson avenue. It was settled largely by poor European immigrants: Englishmen from Cornwall, Scots, Irish, Welsh, French Canadians, Italians, Finns, Swedes, Germans, Poles, Lithuanians, Hungarians, Croats, Serbs, and a sprinkling of Lebanese and Jews, as well as several other nationalities and ethnic groups. The heads of families were primarily employed in the underground iron ore mines. The English, some of whom were second or third generation citizens, tended to hold the better jobs and important positions in the community.

By 1901 Albert was living in Ironwood, on the far west end of the U.P. Ironwood was very similar to Iron Mountain in its ethnic makeup, and was largely dependent on the iron mining industry. Like Iron Mountain, it was a small city with a population of slightly over 9,000 people, mostly European immigrants.

Winter scene at the railroad depot in Ironwood, 1900s.

On August 5, 1904 Albert was cleaning out cinders from the locomotive's furnace as it travelled down the tracks. A gust of wind carried some of the cinders into the face of one Charles M. Clark, who promptly summoned David Foley, an officer of the law, and had Albert arrested for 'assault and battery.' A quick trial was held three days later before Peter Johnson, Justice of the Peace, where he was found guilty.

Albert became a naturalized American citizen on October 3, 1904; his sponsors were Jacob Abraham and Sam J. Khoury of Iron Mountain.[2]

George Albert found an attorney, Julius J. Patek, filed an appeal, and a new trial was held on December 7, 1904. Patek told the court that "there could be no assault by throwing cinder in the direction of the complaining witness unless there

---

[2] Gogebic County Naturalization Record Book 8B, page 10. Albert said he had arrived in this country six years before at age 15, though in fact he was 16 years old in 1904!

was a present ability to hit him." Patek told the Justice of the Peace that "it is undisputed that the distance between Clark and the train was 125 feet." Patek argued that "shooting and throwing are distinct things—while a gun will carry such a distance, human force is not such as can be compared with the discharge of a gun."

The jury upheld the previous verdict; George Albert was fined $10, assessed $56.45 in court costs, and sentenced to sixty days in jail. It was the Albert family's introduction to litigious American society.

By December 7, 1907 Albert was established as a dry goods merchant in Ironwood, operating out of a rented building on Suffolk street, across from the old St. James Hotel. He was part of a tightknit little community of Lebanese who settled in Ironwood, many of whom were peddlers, and former residents of Fih-El-Koura. They had surnames like George, John, Nicholas, Abraham, Khoury, Abdallah, and Hydar.

Many of these immigrants purchased lots in the Megan and Koenig Addition, along what is today Michigan avenue and north to the highway. Religious services were held in their homes until the spring of 1904 when they started St. Simon Orthodox Church at 242 east Harding. The priest for many years was a man named Elias Hamati.

Rev. Nicola Yanney, himself an immigrant from the same village, united George Albert and Lulu Hydar in marriage on September 4, 1910. Albert also joined the Ironwood Chamber of Commerce that year.

Not long after his marriage, Albert felt his business was not developing enough, and decided to close out his store. He was indebted to Lauerman Brothers Company for several hundred dollars; they took him to court in February 1911, asking for $1,000, and were awarded a default judgment in the amount of $515.08, plus court costs.

On January 3, 1911, Albert wrote a letter to another supplier and creditor, J. M. Riegelhaupt of Cleveland, Ohio, stating that "business has been very quiet, [and] I made up my mind to go out of business. I am sending you goods amounting to $226.56 and a check for the balance hoping you will receive them safe. I thought this was the best thing to do so you would not have to wait for the full amount."

A view looking south on Suffolk street, just north of intersection with Aurora. The first Albert store was near the center of the next block, at left.

Albert packed everything up and had it shipped via railroad to Cleveland. Isadore Riegelhaupt received and examined the shipment, finding that there were goods missing, as well as others included that did not belong to them; he took Albert to court in December 1911, suing him for damages. Albert hired attorney Curtis Buck, and the court awarded Riegelhaupt a judgment of $9.06 plus $13 in costs in March 1912.

By 1912 George Albert was in business selling dry goods, shoes and men's furnishings in a building at 128 east Aurora street, rented from John Shea. On August 9, 1916 Albert rented a storeroom at 102 west Aurora street from Hans Everson for one year at an annual rent of $420. On November 29, 1916, Albert had a new lease drawn up to himself and "one Khoury... so that he could be relieved from the further payment of rental."

Looking east on Aurora street, 1900s.

Albert's affairs became more straitened, and he fell behind in rent payments for December 1916 through March 1917, and the first five days of August 1917. Everson went to court on October 13, 1917, and in November was awarded a judgment of $144 plus costs of $40.35. Attorney Belmont Waples represented Albert.

Thus far Albert had been a defendant in four legal actions since settling in Ironwood. It must have been an education in lawyers and American justice for this young Lebanese immigrant.

In May 1914 George Albert made his first real estate purchase, buying lot 5 in Block 10 of Megan and Koenigs 1st Addition. It was located on the south side of what was then Charles street—later renamed Michigan avenue. The lot cost $164. In October 1916 he purchased the adjacent lot 4 for $200; his brother Mose Albert bought lots 2 and 3 in 1916 and 1918 respectively, selling them to him in May 1921 for $3,450. George Albert's modest home was located at 157 Michigan avenue; he resided there until his death almost fifty years later.

Albert made another major purchase of real estate five years later when he bought the building housing the Model Clothing Store at 105-07 south Suffolk street from Maud W. Fehr, widow of Fred Fehr, proprietor of the Davis & Fehr Department Store in Ironwood, for $10,000. A Finnish immigrant named William Maki operated the Model Clothing Store.

Maki had taken a five-year lease on the building in December 1915 for a rent of $85 per month; after Albert purchased the building he raised Maki's rent to $100 per month. Albert, represented by attorney Charles Humphrey Sr., filed a lawsuit against Maki on December 8, 1920, asking for $1,020 per annum rental of the ground floor. Albert said he was owed $170; the case was discontinued three weeks later.

Albert filed a new claim on March 16, 1921, and was awarded $1,226.32 in June 1922. Maki went bankrupt by the summer of 1924, and Albert purchased the inventory of the Model Store at a public sale for $17,600 in April 1925.

In May of 1922 Albert made another big purchase when he bought lot 18 of Block 22 on Aurora street from Jerry F. Shea and other heirs of John J. Shea for $19,000. He remodeled his store on this lot at 128 east Aurora and reopened for business; following Maki's bankruptcy he remodeled the lower floor of his building at 105-07 south Suffolk and sought tenants to rent it. Albert then reopened in a building rented from Hans Everson on the northwest corner of Aurora and Lowell, across the street from the old Curry Hotel.

George Albert eventually owned the buildings at right, near corner.

Albert was doing well enough, and purchased a Willys Knight seven-passenger sedan automobile from car dealer Henry Barr on April 17, 1923 for $2,195. It turned out to be a sour deal, as Albert complained that the self-starter and engine were "defective, broken and improperly constructed;" he could not start the engine unless the car was towed or pushed "for a considerable distance." The automobile, he complained, had a leak in the roof above the front seat, and "in wet weather we have to stop and climb into the back seat to keep from getting wet." Besides that, "the body of the car was loose on the chassis," the "paint was peeled, spotted, streaked and cracked... within a very short time, and the springs came up through the seats." It was a "rattling automobile," he later said, and it cost him $100 for repairs, with no resulting improvement.

George and Lulu Albert leased the east half of the ground floor of their building on Aurora street on January 2,

1925 to George Laggis and Nick Laggis, who operated a confectionary store and ice cream parlor. The five-year lease required a monthly rent of $165, or $9,900 for the full term. Laggis gave up his lease in 1930. The store at 128 east Aurora was again remodeled, and rented to the Great Atlantic and Pacific Tea Company beginning in April 1930 for $445 per month.

Albert hired Waples and Waples, attorneys, and filed suit against the Willys-Overland company on February 3, 1925; the case was dismissed in late November 1925. A new suit was filed against the automobile manufacturer and local agent Harry Barr on April 18, 1925, and subsequently dismissed on November 22, 1926. Albert had sought $1,600 in damages.

George Albert was well-off enough to purchase a $159.50 "cloth coat trimmed with fur" for his wife from the Seaman Brothers clothing store on October 12, 1925. Weeks and months went by as the Seaman Brothers awaited payment; finally they filed suit in August of 1926 asking for $200. Albert responded by claiming the coat was of "poor quality and faded upon becoming wet." An agreement was reached and the lawsuit was dismissed in February 1927.

In October of 1929 one of Albert's little daughters had her eye operated on by Dr. Paul Lieberthal. The doctor allegedly told him that it was "a very simple operation requiring but one suture and no anesthesia." The result was an incision 1-1/2 inches long, made under anesthesia, with at least seven sutures, and lasting one hour. Albert complained that his daughter's cheek had been cut by scissors when the bandage was later removed, and that she could not close her eyelid completely. He was afraid his daughter would be disfigured for life, and kept her home from school for five months following the surgery.

Albert spent $200 on medical bills, and filed a $25,000 lawsuit against Dr. Lieberthal in September 1930. Attorney Edward Massie represented him in what was described as the "only malpractice suit ever tried in Gogebic county" up to that time. The jury deliberated for four hours before acquitting Dr. Lieberthal in December 1931.

In June 1930 Albert leased two rooms on the ground floor of a woodframe building at 100 west Aurora street from Hans Everson, and set up his inventory. The rent at his new location was $150 per month or $1,800 for one year. At some point during the winter the water pipes froze in the bathroom in the back of the building. Albert complained of a foul odor coming from the restroom, and repaired some rotten boards in the floor. He did not like the conditions in the building, and gave up his lease in January 1931. Everson filed suit against Albert in June, claiming backrent, and was awarded a settlement. Everson died shortly after, and Albert was ordered to pay $765 to his estate.

Sometime in 1930 Albert moved his clothing store to the second floor of his building at 105-07 south Suffolk street, where it remained for several years before being moved down to the ground level. The A&P gave up its lease and vacated the building on Aurora street in June 1940, and Albert had to find a new tenant.

In August 1940 the Aurora street building was leased to the Piggly Wiggly Store, operated by Lionel Jacquart and William Dawson, through February 1942 for $300 per month. After they surrendered the lease, Albert was anxious to find a new tenant. He did not want to lease it to local businessmen, because, he said, "I figure they could not pay the rental the building required. For $100 a month, I might as well give them the key and tell them the property is their's."

Albert then began a long negotiation with Montgomery Ward and Gamble Stores in an attempt to convince one or the other to take a lease. Letters were exchanged back and forth for a year before an apparent agreement was reached with Gamble-Skogmo, and a $200-a-month lease was drawn up and signed in April 1944.

The lease required Albert to paint and decorate the inside rooms of the store and plaster the walls in the basement at his own expense, while Albert expected the Gamble Store to add on an addition to the rear of the store, install a stairway to the basement, and make some other improvements at their expense. The first five years rent was set at $200 per month.

Several years later Albert would take Gamble-Skogmo to court over the lease, claiming that he had signed a lease that did not conform to his agreed terms at the time it was drawn up. He hired Solomon W. Patek to represent him, and filed suit in Gogebic County Court on January 24, 1948.

George Albert owned this building on Aurora street.

Albert argued that he had signed a blank lease, which was then filled in afterwards. He told the court he had "just a fair understanding of the English language. I can read common, simple things. I cannot read the complicated legal terminology. My wife, Lulu Albert, is from the same town and country as I am. She has had the same schooling as I have had. I know that of my own knowledge. She and I grew up together. She is my second cousin. She speaks the English language just fair."

George Albert told the court that he would never have agreed to sign the lease had he fully understood the terms set forth in it. Albert lost his case in the local court and appealed to the Michigan Supreme Court in 1951, represented by Patek, with son Theodore G. Albert serving as counsel. The case was dismissed in favor of the defendants in February 1951.

Albert purchased the James George building which adjoined his property on Suffolk street in 1950, and joined the two by an archway, reopening for his 44th anniversary in business on October 10, 1951.

George Albert, about 1940.

George and Lulu Albert were founders of St. Simon Orthodox Church, supporting it all of their lives. He belonged to the Ironwood Lodge No. 149, International Order of Odd Fellows, which met at the Odd Fellow's Hall at 312 south Suffolk, two blocks down from the Albert Store. He was also a member of the Ironwood Lodge No.1278 of the Benevolent and Protective Order of Elks.

One unusual custom Albert and the other Lebanese immigrants brought with them from the old country was smoking the hookah—a water pipe. That was how Albert would relax when he came home from the store.

George Albert's wife Lulu died in 1955. He retired from his clothing business in 1968, suffered from the problems of old age, and died at his home on November 24, 1970. Many of the Albert children had been involved in the store at one time, and his son John Albert took over the business when he retired.

A family of seven sons and three daughters, all of them either college-educated professionals or involved in business, survived George Albert. The elder sons all served in the military during the Second World War, and all had "George" as their middle name.

The Albert Building at left, in August 2008. Ted Albert's law office was upstairs—headquarters of the U.P. 51st State of Superior, Inc. in the 1970s.

2

BIRTH OF A LEGAL CAREER

Theodore George Albert was born in Ironwood, Gogebic county, Michigan on September 26, 1917, the fourth child of George and Lulu Hydar Albert. Ted was an honor roll student, and active in various sports. Attending Central in his elementary school days, he played hockey on the Cubs team before moving up to the Rovers in junior high school.

At some point during his high school career he joined the Kiwani's Key Club, an organization formed in 1930. Local professional men would speak to boys about their professions and offer advice and encouragment. Ted was among two dozen boys who belonged to the club in 1935. He was probably inspired by Solomon W. Patek, a 42-year-old attorney who had an office upstairs in the George Albert building at 107 south Suffolk; Patek was a son of Julius Patek, the lawyer who had defended George Albert back in 1904.

Little is recorded of Ted's high school days because it was during the Great Depression, and no Ironwood High School *Hematite* yearbooks were published in 1935. Following his graduation from Luther L. Wright High School in June 1935 he attended Ironwood Junior College (now known as Gogebic Community College), and served as a stagehand for a play given by the Masquers in December 1936.

Ted, like his brothers, was an avid tennis player during his high school days and beyond. In June 1937 he belonged to the Ironwood Racketeers tennis club, and in one match played against the Ironwood Tennis Club at Ramsay, where he was defeated by Rudy Egizi, the future Gogebic county clerk, 6-4, 6-3. In the spring of 1937 he graduated from Ironwood Junior College with an Associate of Arts degree and enrolled at the University of Wisconsin, where he earned a Bachelor of Arts with majors in history and language.

Ted Albert was married to Marie Mollrud at Winona, Minnesota on October 30, 1941. He graduated from University of Wisconsin Law School with a law degree in June 1942, and went to work as a timekeeper for the Fisher Fleetwood Plant in Detroit. A little later he was promoted to the Fisher Body Division of General Motors Corporation as a Government Regulations Analyst. It was during the Second World War, and he was familiar with over 870 regulations concerning strategic materials like steel, copper, and aluminum.

In the summer of 1944 he was hired by the War Production Board as a Compliance Analyst and Investigator to work in Region 11, in Detroit, Michigan. He had to investigate alleged violations of W.P.B. regulations concerning misuse of 'critical materials, end-products and facilities,' and his supervisor later reported that he "performed all his assignments in a highly capable manner." Due to his knowledge of law, Ted was transferred to the Analysis Section where he studied investigators' reports and recommended closing cases where no violations were found.

Edward J. McKernan, the Regional Compliance Chief, was impressed by Ted and wrote up a nice letter of recommendation, which Ted referred to in political ads years later. In February 1945 he was transferred to naval service as a storekeeper, serving from February 8 to September 13, 1945. He turned down a commission in the United States Navy, and was honorably discharged with rank of Seaman Second Class. Ted returned to Ironwood, securing a position as employment counselor with the United States Employment Service.

In February 1946 he and a group of Ironwood men formed the Northland Sports Organization to "promote and encourage all manly sports and physical culture." Serving as advisor, Ted told the *Ironwood Daily Globe* that the club expected to be an asset to the community. Plans were made for bowling, skiing, trap shooting, basketball, softball, archery, tennis, ping pong, and touch football. In March of that year the club began sponsoring Friday night dances in order to raise funds for its projects, which included the Mount Zion ski hill development.

In May 1946 Ted took and passed the Michigan State Bar exam and was granted his license to practice law the following June 10th. He did not immediately go into practice, but in November 1946 was hired as the area rent attorney or representative for the Office of Price Administration, a federal government wartime organization that was destined to be phased out. The office was located at 219-23 south Suffolk street in Ironwood, a block away from the Albert Store.

Sometime in the spring of 1947 Ted was established in the practice of law, and moved to Room 4 on the second floor of the Albert Building at 105 south Suffolk; he was authorized to practice law in both Michigan and Wisconsin by this time. The earliest court case he was involved in concerned a contractor who had done some landscaping work for one of his brothers. An appeal was filed on September 16, 1947, and there was a stipulative dismissal on May 11, 1948. Another case dating from September 24, 1947 to May 18, 1948 involved an estate that sued the Hamm Brewing Company. Ted's 'opponent' in these suits was prosecuting attorney Bernard Larson.

Ted continued his work as a spokesman and promoter of the Northland Sports Club. In January 1947 he wrote a long letter to the editor of the *Daily Globe* about the club not being allowed to rent the gymnasium at L. L. Wright High School. The Gogebic Ministerial Association had written to the school board to endorse its "policy in prohibiting the Sunday use of the school building."

Some interesting professional ball clubs came to the area on invitation from the Northland Sports Club. The Famous Red Heads womens' basketball club from Missouri appeared in March 1948 when they defeated the Bessemer Merchants 46 to 30 in a game held at the A. D. Johnston Gymnasium in Bessemer. They were invited to return the following month. The Apex Brown Bombers "all Negro football team," Albert Sims, manager, contacted the club in an attempt to fill out its schedule. Jack Rulle, booking manager for the "Bearded Davidites Traveling Baseball Team" and the "Dollyettes Girls Softball Club," contacted the club in June 1948.

In 1948 Ted decided to campaign for the office of Gogebic County Prosecuting Attorney, and ran as a democrat, facing Bernard Larson, the incumbent republican candidate. He had an advantage, because since the Depression and the F. D. Roosevelt administration the county had turned solidly into the democratic camp. After years of republican domination of the county, the voters frequently rejected republican candidates. When the election was held that fall Ted received 6,549 votes to Larson's 5,494. It was Ted's first venture into politics, and the 31-year-old lawyer was on the verge of a long career in the public spotlight.

3

PROSECUTING ATTORNEY

Ted Albert and his family settled in at 111 east Coolidge street in Ironwood in August 1948. He was not the youngest man ever elected to the office of prosecuting attorney in Gogebic County, but he was certainly one of the most intelligent and capable. Soft-spoken and ambitious, he would begin the first of what were to be four two-year terms in January 1949. There were sixteen other lawyers practicing in Gogebic County, which at the time had a population of about 27,000, but Ted at least had a paid position.

His first recorded case as prosecuting attorney involved a man who was sued for non-support; the case was dropped in February 1950. Another case concerned a man who had been pulled over by the Department of Natural Resources at Watersmeet. This gentleman allegedly resisted inspection of his car by a D. N. R. officer, and was arrested and taken to court in February 1949, where he was found not guilty.

Governor G. Mennen Williams appointed Ted to serve as Friend of the Court, and he served until 1953, when he resigned. He became a member of the Prosecuting Attorneys Association of Michigan and was founder of the Prosecuting Attorneys Association of Northern Michigan. Ted belonged to a plethora of organizations, including the National Association of County and Prosecuting Attorneys, the Upper Peninsula Law Enforcement Association, Gogebic-Ontonagon Bar Association, Michigan State Bar Association, Wisconsin State Bar Association, National Association of Claimants' Compensation Attorneys, Michigan Association of Claimants' Compensation Attorneys, American Judicature Society, Lions Club of Ironwood, the Loyal Order of the

Moose Lodge, No. 159, and the Legion of the Moose, No. 127.

Ted's first two terms as Prosecuting Attorney were very busy for him. He had to settle controversies, and sometimes create some of his own. His first major battle involved the Grand View Hospital in Bessemer Township, which was originally built in the 1920s as a tuberculosis sanatorium. It was a public institution, paid for by the taxpayers of Gogebic county.

The hospital board of trustees had written up a number of bylaws that they said the hospital and medical staff had to abide by. One regulation required a doctor to have another doctor present during surgery, and the doctor had to split his fee with the other doctor. Chiropractors and osteopaths were singled out "by special interest groups" and 'restricted and limited' in their practice. There were a number of other rules as well, which eventually led to a dispute as the board tried to impose the regulations upon a dissenting physician.

One of Ted Albert's brothers who was a medical doctor worked on his patients at Grand View. He objected to several of the rules, and especially to the one that forced "fee-splitting." Dr. Albert was barred from the hospital, and his sizeable cliental became incensed at the trustees for denying them the doctor of their choice.

Ex-congressman Frank Hook complained that the former 'mining aristocracy' had 'engineered the hospital to cover up silicosis cases and shift the burden of their care from the mining companies to the state.' In Hook's opinion it was a sort of clever scam on the part of mining companies to force the public to care for men who developed miner's consumption working in the iron mines.[3]

---

[3] Sometime during the controversy Frank Hook went to the hospital for emergency treatment and wanted Dr. Albert to be his physician, but was irked to discover that the Doctor had been banned.

Ted sought an official opinion from Michigan Attorney General Stephen Roth. The resulting thirteen-page document was dated February 24, 1950, and said "The constitution nowhere authorizes the delegation of legislative power to the trustees of a county hospital.... A statute or ordinance purporting to vest an arbitrary discretion with respect to the granting or withholding of licenses, permits, etc., respecting lawful businesses or professions is unconstitutional and void." The trustees of Grand View Hospital were only empowered to make rules "concerning tubercular infection."

In July 1950 Ted secured another letter from the Attorney General clarifying the status of chiropractors. This sixteen-page opinion stated that "an aboriginal witch doctor, tribal medicine man or doctor of voodoo might lawfully practice medicine in this state provided he satisfied the requirements of the basic science act and the medical practice act. This is not said in disparagement of any school of medicine but is merely a statement of the law of this state... A lawfully licensed chiropractor is a legal practitioner of a school of medicine recognized by the laws of Michigan." The Gogebic County Chiropractors placed a large advertisement in the *Daily Globe* thanking the hospital trustees and Ted "for a job well done in procuring Attorney General Roth's opinion."

The Grand View Hospital's rules would have been acceptable had it been a private institution, but as it was a public hospital it could not discriminate against anybody who held a license to practice medicine. The board of trustees were informed of the Attorney General's opinion and adopted a new set of rules, which Ted said, "were the same as the old ones... and automatically invalid."

Doctor Albert's patients "were threatening to force entrance with the use of guns, and the community was riled and incensed by the action" of the board of trustees. One man whose daughter needed to have a tumor operated on and removed by the Doctor, told the Gogebic County Board of Supervisors, "If anything happens to my daughter, I promise you that I will take matters in my own hands. My daughter is going to Grand View and she will have Dr. Albert's services."

Doctor Albert and several of his patients sued, and he won his case against the hospital; when the defendants appealed to the Michigan Supreme Court, it found in his favor, issuing a fourteen-page opinion in December 1954. But the trustees were still not convinced, and the long and bitter dispute was destined to continue into the early 1960s, long after Ted's term as prosecuting attorney had ended.

Ted Albert ran for a second term as Prosecuting Attorney in 1950, defeating republican Robert A. Burns of Wakefield by 892 votes.

On the afternoon of June 2, 1952 there was a sizeable cave-in at the Pabst shaft of the Penokee iron mine in Ironwood that resulted in two fatalities and the temporary entombment of three other miners. It took place north of the former Pabst mine where three men had been killed and 43 trapped for five days back in 1926 when parts of the shaft collapsed and prevented their exit.

The rock to the north of the ore deposit, called the 'hanging wall,' was a type of slate that was prone to cracking, slipping and sliding without much warning. Part of this hanging wall collapsed at the nearby Norrie mine in 1912, crushing seven men. Another close call took place in the Penokee mine in 1942 when two miners were killed in a big collapse; there was a rumble, and somebody managed to sound the alarm; a large number of men fortunately escaped just in time to avoid a massive cave-in.

Such accidents were always dismissed as "acts of God," especially back in the days of mining company rule, which came to an end following the Depression and the rise of the Steelworkers Union. Ted felt there should be an investigation of the Penokee disaster, and called for a coroner's inquest; it was apparently, as he often claimed, the first such inquest ever held in Gogebic county. Of course, there had been many coroner's inquests in the past when men were killed in mining accidents, but never one that lasted for days and attracted such attention.

MINE TRAGEDY—The body of Jorma Oikonen, 33, one of two men killed in the cavein at the Penokee mine, was brought to the surface at 11:30 p. m. yesterday. (Daily Globe photo)

Within two days of the cave-in the federal mine inspector and his county counterpart both told the newspaper that the Penokee mine was not unsafe, and had "no serious hazards," an assessment that appears to have been based principally upon the local average of 'lost time accidents' compared to the national average for mines; the accident was "a natural hazard in mining and the result of what might be called some careless underground housekeeping by Mother Nature," reporters were told.

This part of the Gogebic Range mining district was notorious for such catastrophic events; past operations in this stretch of ground had demonstrated that continued mining was akin to a game of Russian roulette, and Ted evidently believed there needed to be more than a perfunctory inquest that merely brushed it off as being 'incidental or unavoidable to the business of mining.'

Several miners complained that they had been expecting something to happen for weeks before the accident; that men were having premonitions and "funny feelings." One man was told by his mine captain, "If you don't like it you can go home." This miner called the operations "butcher shop mining."

On the evening of June 16, 1952 a group of six local businessmen and miners met with Ted Albert and Theodore Nyman, the county mine inspector, at the Memorial Building in Ironwood. About a dozen miners gave their testimony. There was also an audience of close to 300 people seated in the auditorium, and the session lasted for four hours—almost until midnight.

Miners had noticed cracks in the ore in the area of the cave-in before it collapsed. One miner told the inquest, "I didn't see the safety man for the last three months in our work place." Another told of watching pieces of earth drop down —"dribbling"—before the collapse, and falling chunks, often a sign of an impending cave-in.

The inquest panel met again the following evening; another session was held on a Friday night and lasted until 3 o'clock in the morning. The panel was split on a verdict, four to two. Ralph Rowell and Reino Laine, the former an ex-democratic representative, miner and miners' union organizer, the latter a miner and future mine inspector, probably voted to find the Penokee Ore Company negligent. The other four men on the panel, local businessmen, may have been split; some were probably inclined to find the accident was an unavoidable act of God.

Ted sent a 400-page transcript of the inquest to Governor Williams, asking him to appoint a special committee to investigate the disaster.

In October the Gogebic County Board issued a statement deploring 'inquests being held where none are necessary,' and requesting coroners "to refrain from holding unnecessary inquests, as they are a needless expense to the county."

Ted took the board to task, explaining to them that inquests were not ordered by coroners, but by prosecuting attorneys. "There was not a needless inquest held. Any money spent to determine the question of how a man died is money well spent... As a result of the Penokee inquest, contracts now contain safety clauses that are better than before, and the inquest resulted in legislation that will be a benefit for years to come."

As Prosecuting Attorney of Gogebic County, Ted Albert made an effort to establish the "powers of elective office holders and returned to them all of the powers unlawfully taken away," giving "respect and purpose to their offices." In November 1952 he presented his opinion on the Mine Inspector's powers to the County Board. He informed them that the Mine Inspector had the power to appoint up to three deputy inspectors.

Miners at the Sunday Lake mine in Wakefield went on a wildcat strike on February 13, 1952 to protest the unsafe practice of having a "three-man two-place gang." Ted convinced the Mine Inspector, Theodore Nyman to issue an order requiring two men at every work place. Nyman said the old practice was "careless," and all of the local mines immediately complied with his order, the miners returning to work three days later.

Ted's work on behalf of miners included compiling and updating the United Steelworkers of America *Workmen's Compensation Law* booklet. He also held inquests into hunting fatalities, and claimed his efforts led to state action to protect hunters and enforce laws.

Just before the 1952 election for county offices, all of the candidates delivered radio addresses. Ted complained that his opponent was spreading lies; "In his last radio broadcast he deliberately and falsely read to you in part from a letter he claims that I wrote to the Justice Courts and Justices telling them to dispense with arraignments and with the right of accused individuals to have attorneys. There is no such letter... he made it up with all his guts and gall."

Ted's opponent in the 1952 election was Clifford Trethewey, whom he defeated 7,162 to 6,194, winning a third term as prosecuting attorney.

During this time Ted continued his interest in sports, and was the manager of the Gogebic Rangers semi-professional football team, as well as the Gogebic Rangers basketball team. He also managed and sponsored softball teams from 1948 to 1956, and was elected president of the Northland Sports Club in 1953.

In April 1953 Ted ran for Circuit Court Judge but was trounced by incumbent Thomas J. Landers in the primary election, 7,088 to 2,518.

During the summer of 1953 a minor controversy arose over bingo games and charitable raffles in the county, with articles appearing in the local newspaper. Ted was asked to comment on the issue, and told the *Daily Globe* that as long as the money derived was "used for a charitable, fraternal, non-profit and good purpose there [would] be no enforcement of the lottery law. Unless commercial or private interests become involved I will no more seek out charitable games and raffles than I would seek out sociable poker games and fortune telling which are also illegal in the state of Michigan."

In 1954 Ted ran against Clifford Trethewey, and was re-elected to a fourth and final term as prosecuting attorney, narrowly defeating Trethewey 5,968 to 5,638. His final two-year term as prosecuting attorney was over at the end of 1956.

In January 1957 a permanent injunction was issued against the Grand View Hospital board to prevent them from interfering with Dr. Albert's medical practice. The 1948 staff rules and 1950 bylaws were ordered not to be enforced. In April 1958 Frank Drazkowski, superintendent of Grand View Hospital, brought charges against Dr. Albert and his brother James Albert, a podiatrist. In order to fulfill one of the hospital's rules, Dr. James Albert had been present during surgeries performed by his brother. They were charged with violation of "a state act governing issuing of licenses for practice of medicine and surgery." The Doctor felt the purpose of the action was to "deprive him of his license to practice medicine and surgery anywhere."

Dr. Albert was readmitted to the hospital's medical staff in January 1960, but his privileges were again revoked in June. The hospital trustees ran a "Public Notice" in the newspaper announcing the fact that he was not allowed to admit or treat patients. Dr. Albert began a $12,000,000 civil rights suit against Frank Drazkowski et alia, which included Gogebic County as a defendant.

Ted led the group of patients and supporters who were trying to get the county board to intervene on Dr. Albert's behalf. The county board continued to refuse to intervene in the controversy despite their authority to do so. In late June of 1960 the Doctor's supporters pressed the board for a special hearing for their petition requesting his reinstatement; the movement continued for the following two years.

In November 1962 Ted composed a lengthy "Statement of Public Interest" about the hospital controversy. It included a copy of a letter written by four county supervisors urging that the board give the group a full hearing. Dr. Albert offered to drop the county from his lawsuit if it reinstated him to the hospital with full privileges. The Doctor's supporters had gathered petitions with 2,500 signatures asking for his reinstatement, and the county board finally voted to reinstate him, but only on a probationary basis.

Ted wrote in part:

The history of the controversy in every court case proves that Dr. Albert has been right on the rules. Dr. Albert has been right on the law and Dr. Albert has defended successfully against false charges. It isn't likely he is off base now.

We have heard that this County Board is trying to keep expenses down in the County, yet when they have an opportunity to avoid a very expensive law suit, they refuse to do so. Why?

...I hope that some of this will be the impetus to some good toward our common welfare. No person, born and raised in Gogebic County or area, could but have an earnest and sincere hope for the successful future of our community. We, here in the Upper Peninsula, have much to sell, much to advertise, all truly emanating not from man made objects but from our bountiful God given natural resources. All this we have but find it difficult to promote because of man made resistances. I firmly believe that our existing social ideas in this community—our conduct in relation to one another has the most telling effect on our economic and political future. Our community, bearing more churches than most and presumably as Christian and God loving as any other, finds itself mired in the stigma of wholly un-Christianlike, ungodly acts. People of our community, having all the complexes which result from narrow minded bigotry and selfishness, find ways to rationalize and reconcile even the most uncommon and un-Christianlike acts.

In our community, men and women of learning and education have used it not for leadership, understanding or compassion, but to exact punishment, penalties, deprivation or whatever vindictive act satisfies their un-Christianlike souls. These same people have kept from the citizens at large the true facts and all that would enlighten them on the subjects of interest and concern and those subjects that might cause them to act concertedly.

I have been told not to speak out. I have been counseled that it is wiser to be hurt and wait. I have been told that I will only arouse the opposition, make them more active, more vindictive. I can no longer heed this advice. I feel it is the time to talk—the time to challenge—to get to the very core of the boil that gnaws, draws and contracts at the very heart of our community.

Who can cause Dr. Albert, his family and the entire Albert family more hurt or anguish than has been exacted? What is it that the Alberts' owe this community? What is the name of the crime that comes from our simple demand to live here—peaceably in safety and security?[4]

In later years Ted often pointed out that negative and misleading publicity generated by his brother's antagonists in connection with the hospital controversy, which provoked his own forceful and successful defense of the Doctor, had created animosity and had a negative effect on his subsequent political career.

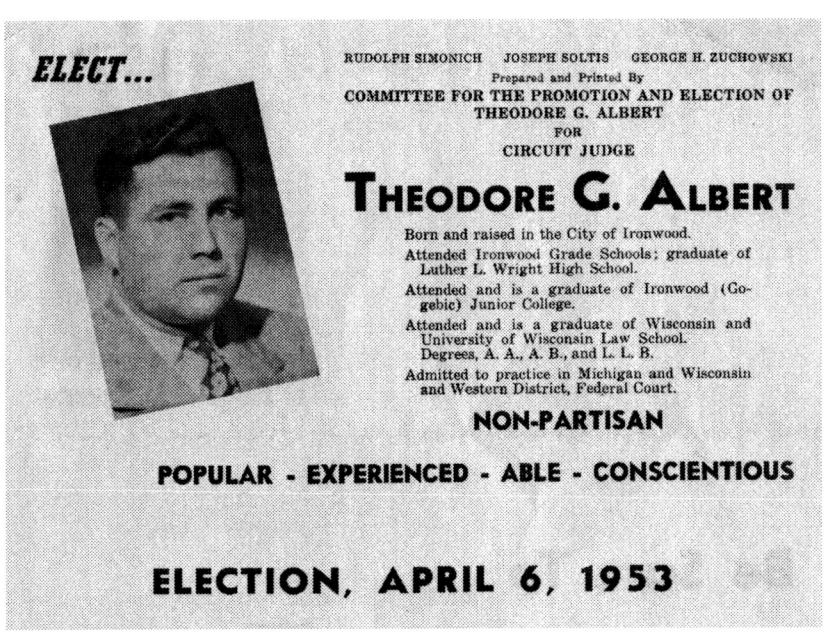

---

[4] "A Statement of Public Interest, November 23, 1962."

4

DEMOCRATIC DISSENTERS

Ted Albert was very active in the democratic party; he served as a delegate to all of the county and state conventions, and was cited and commended for his work in elections and recounts. He told the voters that he was "diligent in attendance at all district meetings," and that he formulated and prepared "resolutions and correspondence for the democratic party." In 1951 he served as Sergeant at Arms at the Democraic National Convention.

Democratic party leaders convinced Ted to run for Congress in 1956, and he was one of four candidates who ran for the democratic nomination. Ted came in third with 4,039 votes, while Frank Hook received 6,877 and Joe Mack, 7,741. It was only sometime later after the election that he learned why the party was so anxious to have him in the running:

Party leaders were not interested in me or my qualifications or capabilities. Their only interest was to defeat another qualified candidate, Frank E. Hook. They were intent on defeating Frank E. Hook for reasons only known to them. Everyone knows that I did not campaign on the theory that I must assassinate anyone's character or that I must libel and slander any candidate. I did not refer in any of my speeches or radio talks to Joseph S. Mack, Frank E. Hook, or William J. Bolognesi.

I didn't believe that any of the candidates in the field would partake in slurring lies one against the other. There was one candidate who did lie and on such a widespread scale—it has taken me two years to catch up to all of the malicious lies that were told. It was the only way that he could explain my candidacy to the voters—certainly to overcome my qualifications and his lack of them. I want the voters of the Twelfth District to have no doubts about my feelings and I would be remiss in my duties as a citizen if I did not convey this information to you.

Joseph Mack was Hook's campaign manager in 1954 when Hook ran for state representative and lost; Mack became interested in politics and ran in 1956, winning the primary but losing the election that November; Mack was finally elected to the state legislature in 1960, and would remain in office for the following twenty-six years. If Ted had not run in the 1956 primary, chances are good that Hook would have received many of the votes that were cast for him, and could have defeated Joe Mack.

In his 1956 campaign ad, Ted Albert stated he "had an active, participating role in local, state and national party affairs." So it may have come as a shock to local democrats when Ted and some fellow party members of like mind 'rebelled' against the party in 1958, setting up their own new and reformed democratic club.

Some of the U.P. democrats were being pushed aside by the party in Lower Michigan. Frank E. Hook, a native of L'Anse and former resident of Wakefield and later Ironwood, served as a representative from Michigan to the United States Congress from 1935 to 1943 and 1945 to 1947. Hook was a close friend of President Harry Truman, and if Alben Barkley had not accepted Truman's offer of the vice presidency in 1948, Hook would have been his next choice.

Hook ran for senator in 1948 and was snubbed by the democratic party elites. In the book *Fightin' Frank, The Biography of Upper Peninsula's 12th District Democratic Congressman*, by his daughter, Mary Hook Allen, she writes that her father would not go along with the socialistic element of the party, headed by Neil Staebler. During an election rally held in Ypsilanti, when Hook was not present to see what was going on, this cadre snubbed him, not even mentioning his name as a candidate. But Mary Hook happened to be in the crowd and reported the snub to her father.

Labor union honchos had tried to pressure Truman into not endorsing Hook's senatorial candidacy, but the president refused to listen to them. It turned out to be a very close race, possibly complicated by election fraud, but Hook did not contest the results. Another opportunity opened up with the death of Arthur H. Vandenberg, the Michigan senator, in April 1951. Governor Williams promised Hook the vacant position. Once again the clique attacked Hook, whispering in the governor's ear; Williams reneged on his promise. Seeds of ill will had been planted and would ripen seven years later in the U.P.

By the beginning of 1958 Ted Albert and Frank Hook got together with William L. Johnson, general manager of WJMS radio in Ironwood, and discussed the state of affairs in Michigan. They all agreed that the AFL-CIO, especially the United Auto Workers, led by Walter Reuther, dominated Governor Williams.

They all felt there was a socialist / communist cadre at work in the Michigan democratic party, and that Neil Staebler and Gus Scholle were among the ringleaders. Staebler was by then serving on the Michigan State Democratic Central Committee; his friend Gus Scholle, was president of the Michigan AFL-CIO.

More disgruntled democrats from the Lower Peninsula joined the group. Homer Martin, a minister and former UAW president, had once run for Congress as a republican. In 1957 he led a strike by dairy farmers against major Detroit milk dealers.

Martin told a newspaper that Walter Reuther was involved in "political unionism," and was the "captor and captive of the Democratic Party... Reuther allows 15-cent-an-hour auto workers in Europe to drive UAW members into unemployment." In another interview he told a reporter that democrats were "up against Marxian socialists who now sit squarely astride the Democratic machine in the state."

Michael T. Mohardt was a former deputy state securities commissioner who began his political career in 1932 as a precinct delegate in the democratic party. He served as a circuit court clerk in Wayne county and was a former employee of United States Steel Corporation and the Ford Motor Company.

Mohardt was very active in the party, and ran unsuccessfully for Congress in 1942. Governor Van Wagoner fired him from his position as a securities commissioner for running against Representative John Lesinski. Following his run for Congress he was a self-employed merchandise and real estate dealer.

In 1958 Mohardt said, "The democratic party in Michigan has deteriorated into a communist-socialist combine... No candidate can run without getting the okay of someone. If a man runs without the okay of the clique, he is classified as anti-labor."

Norton N. Wisok, a Detroit lawyer and former prosecuting attorney for Wayne county, had been acquainted with Ted Albert for some time. Wisok was in agreement with Ted and the other democratic 'rebels' about Governor Williams and the labor unions.

The men got together and formed "The State Democratic Club of Michigan," which they incorporated on February 14, 1958. Wisok was president and director, with Hook serving as vice president, Ted Albert as secretary, and Mohardt as treasurer. Johnson was one of three trustee / directors, along with Anthony Grendatti of Calumet and Jack Jetty of Iron Mountain. The headquarters was listed as 105 Suffolk street in Ironwood—Ted's law office.

The purpose of The State Democratic Club of Michigan was to "advance the interests of the true Democrats in the Democratic Party for its general welfare and prosperity and growth throughout the state of Michigan in each county thereof." Stationary was prepared with a letterhead depicting the capital building at Lansing. Peter Martinac was added to the list of directors, and applications for membership were mailed to local democratic organizations around the state.

Already by early February the Democratic Central Committee had become aware of the new club and sent letters to all of the county chairmen, as well as to Neil Staebler, and drawn up a response to the rebels:

It is saddening to hear people like Mr. Hook and Mr. Johnson, who in their hearts know better, repeat the moth-eaten Republican charges of CIO-domination and socialistic trends in the Democratic party.

The fact that some Republicans also are again playing the same stale political record raises an interesting question:

Are Republican coins feeding both nickelodeons?

The new group met at the DAV Hall in Detroit in early April 1958 and nominated candidates for office. Michael Mohardt told the 100 persons in attendance, "This organization is for people who want to do more than vote. It will serve as a forum for all democrats." William Johnson was nominated to run for governor, and said the "walls of the palace guard of the state democratic organization must be stormed by the hosts of courage, morality and of vision... We stand shoulder to shoulder, unafraid of the ugly truth and half-truth of the demagog."

Charles M. Diggs of Detroit, who was elected to the Michigan legislature and served from 1955 to 1958, also attended the nominating convention, telling the audience that the "democratic party in Michigan is ruled by fear and the threat of reprisal."[5]

Homer Martin was nominated to run for the United States Senate against Philip Hart, and Hook was nominated as candidate for the United States House of Representatives, while Mohardt was the club's candidate for lieutenant-governor.

---

[5] This was an elder man named Charles Diggs, not the younger man who served in the U.S. Senate and resigned from office about 1998.

Hook was Governor Williams' bitterest foe. Standing on the platform, supporting himself with two canes, he told newsmen that Williams was leading Michigan...

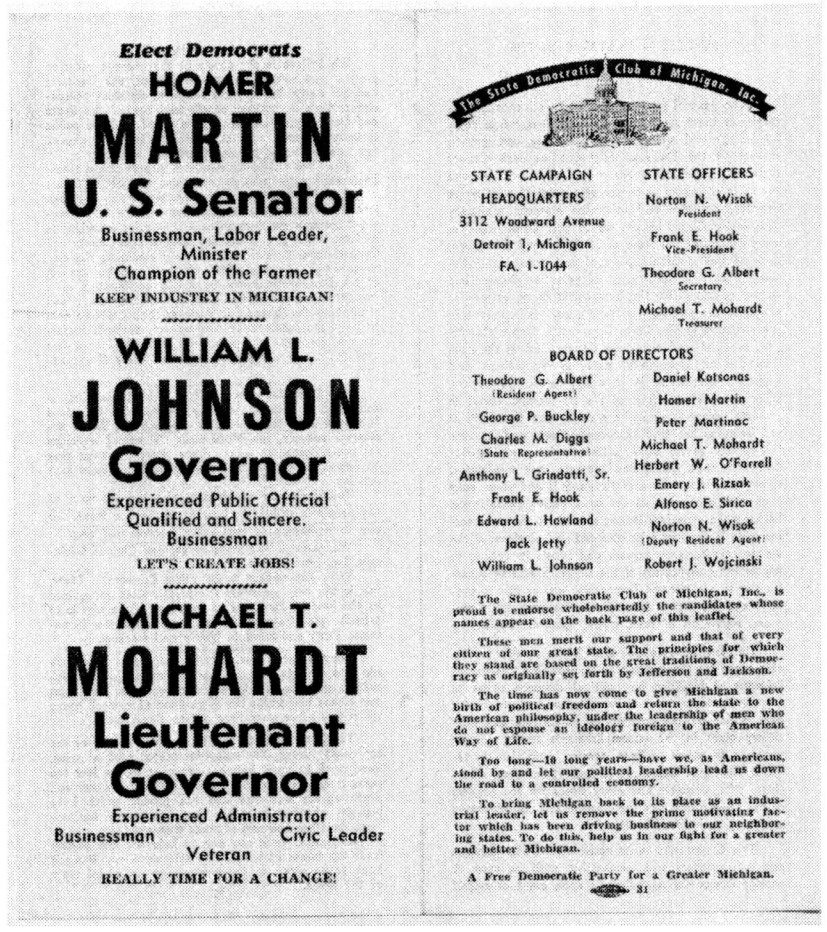

...down the road to national socialism... I will debate G. Mennen Williams on any platform in the state if he denies that Gus Scholle calls the shots in state government and Walter Reuther gives the orders.

I attended a meeting of the Union for Democratic Action in Washington where they changed their name to Americans for

Democratic Action at my suggestion. Reuther, Scholle and George Edwards were in attendance. The Americans for Democratic Action discussed plans for achieving a national-socialist government by 1960; I got up and walked out. We must give the democratic party back to the democrats and the labor unions back to the working men!

William L. Johnson, Theodore G. Albert and Frank E. Hook, 1958.

Neil Staebler was later quoted in a newspaper report, saying, "The State Democratic Club was formed by dissidents and disgruntled office seekers." In late April the United Steelworkers of America passed a resolution claiming the State Democratic Club of Michigan was collaborating with the republicans, and asked it to "cease and desist... and dissolve the club or identify it with a more honest name."

William Johnson told the *Detroit News*,

We are not surprised at the defamatory and uncalled for resolution passed by the Steelworkers from the Upper Peninsula. Governor Williams was a guest speaker at the conference of this group when the resolution was adopted.

This political attack smacks of the political machine built by August Scholle, Walter P. Reuther and their stooge in the governor's chair.

It is action such as this that led to formation of the state democratic clubs.

The club will keep fighting under the banner of the democratic party and will bring the party back to the democrats, free from the taint of any 'ism' except American-ism.

We are preparing a statement requesting a complete public retraction of this libelous and defamatory resolution from the individuals responsible, and the union. If it is not forthcoming, legal action will be started in Federal Court. These smear artists must be stopped for the good of labor and the public.

An anonymous letterwriter with an elementary grasp of the written language and grammar wrote out a two-page missive in pencil, mailing it to William Johnson. It was threatening in tone, with shades of blackmail implied, though whether it was entirely serious or not is open to question. The writer asked Johnson to...

check out these charges from Detroit and then explain in the Voice of the people in the Daily globe, Also you can same time explain why you was fired as City manager from Ironwood and from the Chamber of Commerce... I had lot of respect for you before when I lived in Ironwood but when you turned out to be a traiter to the democratic party in this district and sold out to the Republicans I will work against youse and expose youse to the public Governor Williams is an honest to the people in his state Yours Ex, friend.

Ted Albert prepared a flyer to send out, listing the entire slate of Democratic Club candidates on the front cover, and its purpose, along with a "general comment" on the inside. A campaign headquarters was rented in June 1958 at 3112 Woodward avenue in Detroit. At the primary election held in August, Johnson received 65,614 votes to Williams's 385,864; Martin got 73,334 to Hart's 297,767, and Mohardt received 72,542 to Swainson's 267,670. The State Democratic Club's candidates thus received approximately 20 per cent of the democratic vote, and touted it as a bargaining chip when they sought official recognition from the democratic party at the convention held in Grand Rapids.

REBEL DEMOCRATIC LEADERS MEET

Four leaders of the State Democratic Club of Michigan, Inc. confer here Wednesday during the group's first convention. Shown are (left to right) Herbert W. O'Farrell, board of directors member; Michael T. Mohardt, treasurer; Norton N. Wisok, president, all of Detroit; and Theodore G. Albert of Ironwood, secretary. The club will seek recognition at the Democratic State convention meeting in Grand Rapids Saturday. (Herald Photograph)

The State Democratic Club held its own convention at the Morton House in Grand Rapids on August 23, 1958. It claimed to have close to 15,000 members, and demanded representation on the party ticket in the upcoming election. Wisok donated $13,000 to the club's coffers in order keep up with expenses and the $200 a month rent for its headquarters in Detroit. He told the *Detroit News* that only $36 had been spent on William Johnson's campaign, nothing on the Homer Martin campaign, and $576 on Mohardt's. In two years' time, club members said, the people would probably be fed up enough with Governor Williams to vote for a different governor.

The State Democratic Club of Michigan had a brief existence before disappearing from the political scene. Its members were not the only ones concerned about big labor and Walter Reuther, and that fall there was a fullpage ad in the *Wall Street Journal* about "The Peril of Reuther" and the threat to constitutional government posed by union-control of the United States Congress.

Ted Albert made one last run for prosecuting attorney, garnering 1,626 votes versus 3,626 for William Pellow and 2,384 for Jerome Nadolney, in the August 1958 democratic primary. William Johnson eventually became involved in the republican party, playing a big part in George Romney's successful campaign for governor in 1962. Hook retired from politics, and Wisok later became Ted's law partner in Detroit.

5

TRIALS

The years of the mid-20th century were hard times for the Gogebic Iron Range. Iron mines closed down one after another during the 1950s. There was a major Steelworkers strike in 1959 that lasted for almost half-a-year, and within eight years all of the remaining iron mines were closed. The local economy had been highly dependent upon the iron mines for jobs, and the area entered a period of economic depression.

Many citizens felt the state and federal government were not doing enough to help the iron mines and the U.P., although there was little that could be done to keep underground mines in business in the face of modern taconite production. High tariffs on iron ore imports may have proven no more than a temporary aid.

As somebody closely involved in local politics, Ted was keenly aware of the problems faced by the populace. He wrote a long letter in November 1959 concerning a possible injunction against the striking Steelworkers. He did not approve of the Taft-Hartley Act, qualifying his dislike by stating,

I am not trying to say everything in the Taft Hartley Act is wrong—it isn't. It is my opinion that this act was born out of bias and political inspiration and that it has not improved labor relations.

When and if the new law is written, there must be an absolute rejection of the labor injunction... The present law provides for an injunction which stops the collective bargaining process in its tracks by a court order. We cannot say we are against compulsion and then on the other hand that the Taft Hartley Act is a good law. The Taft Hartley Act compels men to work under court injunction for 80 days on terms they have rejected. I cannot see where there would be any greater compulsion than this.

At some point in 1959 Ted filed a mock bill of complaint for a divorce in federal court, asking for a separation of the Upper Peninsula from Lower Michigan:

Defendant has committed acts of non-support, cruel and inhuman treatment, and subjected the plaintiff to great shame and mental suffering, and on occasions too numerous to mention, accused plaintiff without cause or justification of failing to properly provide for the home of the parties hereto; defendant has claimed the plaintiff is too distant, too cold, too unwieldy, too hard to handle, and for that reason deprives plaintiff of any warm and close association.

Plaintiff and defendant have had financial troubles, and, although plaintiff has warned and cautioned defendant not to spend money foolishly and not to increase unreasonably the cost of maintaining the home of the parties, defendant has refused to listen and shows lack of attention or consideration.

This was the beginning of Ted Albert's movement to turn the U.P. into the 51st State of Superior. Ted was then associated with Robert and Norton Wisok at 1027 Penobscot Building, Detroit, in the practice of law, though his office was maintained at 105-7 Suffolk in Ironwood, from 1958 to 1960. One of the cases Ted handled while in partnership with Wisok was the defense of two brothers who had produced a number of fake income tax returns, claiming about $250,000 in income tax refunds.

In April 1960 Ted's brother, whose long dispute with the Grand View Hospital was still ongoing, filed a $12,000,000 lawsuit against some public officials and doctors in Gogebic County. Ted Albert and Peter Bradt served as attorneys in Dr. Albert's lawsuit. A hearing was set for August 1, 1960, at Marquette, Michigan. The District Judge, W. Wallace Kent, expected to receive a brief from them by July 1st, but the date slipped by without them realizing the significance.

About two weeks later the telephone rang in Bradt's office. It was Judge Kent from Lower Michigan asking where the brief was; the Judge told Bradt there would be no hearing unless a brief were filed, and Bradt replied, "Then there would be no point in us going to Marquette."

Clowning around with the Mounties, 1959.

Judge Kent answered, "That's about the size of it. When we write and ask for briefs, we expect to get some sort of an answer, gaddamit; not have our letters ignored."

Bradt immediately felt offended, and asked, "Judge, would you mind stepping out of this case?"

A longer exchange took place, the Judge informing Bradt, "If you want any disqualification, you file a motion for it."

More discussion took place, Bradt apologizing; five days later he filed his affidavit requesting Judge Kent to be replaced by another judge.

According to Bradt's affidavit, three of the defendants in the case were close personal friends of the Judge, all attorneys; they all belonged to the same political party as the Judge, which they took a prominent part in. Bradt felt their relationship was simply too close for an impartial trial and judgment.

When the day of reckoning arrived, Ted and his partner sat at their table and heard the court declare that Bradt's affidavit 'was not legally sufficient,' denying the motion to have Judge Kent removed. Bradt arose to object and was ordered to be seated. He then asked to be excused from further participation in the case, and was refused. Bradt then got up and walked out, and somebody was sent to bring him back. Ted then got up and walked out, and another lawyer was dispatched to bring him back into the court. The lawyer was not familiar with Ted, and the Judge explained, "Mr. Albert is the dark gentleman sitting in the first chair, who left last."

The Judge charged both Ted and Bradt with contempt of court; they appealed to the higher court, where they lost in September 1961 and were fined.

Michigan was on the verge of holding a constitutional convention in 1961, and Ted wanted to be among the 144 delegates who forged the new document. His legal career was still coming along, and in 1961 he began serving the first of three terms as a Gogebic County Court Commissioner. He announced his candidacy in early July, and issued a long press release, stating in part,

It is imperative that we elect delegates who know the district and its problems. Our delegate must be a person who has understanding of the provisions of our three previous constitutions, including what may have been deleted in the past which was intended to inure to the benefit of our district.

Not one word, not one phrase, not one interpretation should be permitted to find its way into the constitution which would be detrimental to the interests of our district.

I need not remind that we in this district have tellingly felt the full impact of economic distress. We have been disturbed and shocked, with ever growing awareness, for the need of the full utilization of our natural resources. With future welfare in mind, each of us must recognize how necessary and important it is to attract new and diversified industry. We have learned to abhor an economy almost wholly dependent on one major industry. No other district in Michigan has had such a similar problem and no other district has been so affected.

Ted ended his appeal with, "The delegates must have knowledge concerning our organized society, our law, our order, our property, our personal freedom and our political liberty. Important too, is a knowledge of the safeguards against all of the encroachments of tyranny."

Many men campaigned that summer for the primary election, which took place on July 25, 1961. One of them, John Penttila, noted in his campaign ad, "Among the many groups calling for the convention are those who want to do away with township government, to consolidate small city government and centralize county government. This can result in a dictatorship if allowed to happen. It has even been suggested that the Upper Peninsula be one big county."

William Johnson, the former gubernatorial candidate who ran under the banner of the State Democratic Club in 1958, now ran for democratic delegate to the constitutional convention. One of the big issues he took note of in his ad was reapportionment. "Should the legislature be distributed on a strict population basis, thus giving undoubted control to the metropolitan Detroit area... Should the Senate represent area and the House population with some guarantee of representation for sparsely-populated rural and northern areas?"

In the primary election held in July, William Pellow won the vote with 2,936, defeating Ted Albert, who had 1,730. Johnson received 1,748 votes, losing to Frank Perlich of Bessemer who had 1,895.

As the big election approached in September, the *Daily Globe* warned, "The election is especially important to the people of the Upper Peninsula, for if proponents of legislative reapportionment win, the Upper Peninsula will lose representation in the legislature and in Congress." The U.P., already down on its luck, was facing more blows to its dignity. Pellow and Perlich were both elected in September on the democratic ticket. A few weeks later the convention was convened in Lansing.

A new constitution was adopted in 1963, and reapportionment went through. The U.P. and northern part of Lower Michigan lost representation, while power was concentrated in fifteen out of 83 counties, all located in southern Michigan; these fifteen counties held half of the seats in the state legislature: 55 of 110 House seats and 19 of 38 Senate seats.

Reapportionment provided another impetus for the 51st statehood movement. Politicians from the U.P. had always been little fish in a big pond, and now there were even fewer little fish. The statehood movement heated up again, and an informal group headed by Robert Wylie of Sault Ste. Marie met at the Travelers Hotel in St. Ignace. Separate statehood funded by legalized gambling was at the center of the agenda.[6]

Ted may well have either attended the meeting or heard of it. He sat down one day in 1962 and wrote up in pencil what amounted to a declaration of U.P. independence:

We the people of the Upper Peninsula of Michigan, __ _____, 1962, in conformity with established precedent, believing that the time has arrived when our present political and economic conditions ought to cease and the right to self government be as-

---

[6] *Marquette Mining Journal*, March 9, 1962, "Upper Peninsula Independence Movement Renewed By Group Pushing For Legalized Gambling."

serted; and availing ourselves with said established precedent and all that entitles us to admission as a separate state, upon conditions which have been fulfilled, do by our delegates, in convention assembled, mutually agree to form ourselves into a free and independent state, by the style and title of the "State of Superior" and do ordain and establish the following constitution for the government of the same."

Details of the constitution were not recorded, but on the back of this declaration Ted jotted down some notes about the first state constitutional convention held in 1835, in which the Bill of Rights stated "All political power is inherent in the people. Government is instituted for the protection, security and benefit of the people; and they have the right at all times to alter or reform the same, and to abolish one form of government and establish another when the public good requires it."

Ted maintained a law office at 517 Jefferson avenue in Stambaugh from 1961 to 1963. During that time he took on a client who was having problems with a property line dispute, a fateful case which later initiated a long string of problems for him.

Ted was still trying to gain another elective office. In late 1963 he produced a brief autobiography for the Michigan Collection of the State Library, stating in part,

If I would point out the things in my career I would point to a day by day realization that the common citizenry is dependent on the capability and loyalty of those who hold public office. It is my opinion that the common man so short-changed by public officials never has his voice heard, in effect, and finds no recourse, but to be totally subservient to whatever the conduct might be on the part of the so-called public servants.

I am one of the founders of the State Democratic Club of Michigan, whose sole intent and purpose was to create a liaison relation between the rank and file party member to the official party machinery. In effect, to create a forum for that individual who held no office, belonged to no committee and was not and could not be a delegate within the scope of the official machinery. I have many writings on this subject, much of which planning was accepted elsewhere but not acknowledged.

He ran for Representative to the United States Congress in the 1964 primary, announcing his candidacy on June 6 of that year. Ted's press release said,
Unless there is a new and vitalized leadership at the Congressional helm, we can expect no more than what the District has obtained in the last 15 to 20 years.
Under the Republican leadership provided this District by the incumbents of old, that now oppose each other, we have doddled along believing that nothing could be done to alleviate a stagnant status quo. Abundant with natural and human resources, we have not found our representative to match it with energetic and constant drive. The district is entitled to action of a positive nature, without any exceptions. The high average of literacy of the people who comprise our district is nationally recognized. The work skills and aptitudes of our people is much recognized and much publicized.
The natural resources are of such abundance that no one can adequately estimate their extent or value. Considered as a product, our District has much to offer in the plus factors, yet, nevertheless, it hasn't been sold, because it is obvious that it hasn't been offered to those who would offer us economic security through the establishment of industry. There continues to be senseless unemployment problems, yet solutions are present...

When the primary election took place, Raymond Clevenger of Sault Ste. Marie won the democratic nomination with 13,256 votes to Ted's 8,005. Following this, another in a string of political defeats, Ted went to Detroit. Robert Wisok retained him to work on a federal case, Wisco Aluminum versus Alsco Aluminum et alia, in 1964. In October 1964 he began working for the lawfirm of Goldfarb and Hudnut in the Guardian Building, while still maintaining his office in Ironwood.

In June 1965 he was appointed to represent two indigent men who were being prosecuted by the state. He filed papers and worked on their cases until February 1966 when he left Goldfarb and Hudnut, leaving disposition of the cases to the firm. Two years later, in November 1968, he was ordered to appear before the court in Lansing; it blamed him for the lack of progress in the cases. Ted explained what he had done, the fact that he had left the employ of the firm, but the court would not accept his explanation, and fined him for contempt.

It was just the beginning of a series of cases that went before the State Bar Grievance Board. The Fittante, Dogans and Pitts cases resulted in fines totalling $500, but not before Ted carried out a long fight. He questioned the Court of Appeals jurisdiction to initiate contempt proceedings, claiming he was denied due process of law. He questioned the lawfulness of the fine assessed against him on May 15, 1969, and the order of May 21, 1969 requiring him to file a brief on the Fittante case within three weeks.

He told the Michigan Supreme Court that he had "fulfilled all of his duties in regard to Fittante. The Court," he said, "was being oppressive to say that [he was] in contempt and to do so in the face of a most satisfied client." Fittante had "advised the Court of his satisfaction and withdrawn miscalculated previous criticism," he told them. The Grievance Board dismissed the Fittante contempt charge in October 1970.

Ted remained in Detroit for a period of time, working in the offices of S. James Clarkson who later became a district judge. Ted was hoping for and expecting an appointment to a position with the federal government, but it never came through.

Soon after leaving the employ of Goldfarb and Hudnut he was divorced. He moved out of his former home on Coolidge street in Ironwood in August 1966, settling in Stambaugh. On October 27, 1967 he married Dorothy Beauchamp, nee Sobotta, in Detroit.

He led a peripatetic existence all during his career in Detroit, which continued up until about 1970, sometimes living out of suitcases in motels, and moving from one place to another. The Pick Fort Shelby, Sheraton Cadillac, Embassy, Parkcrest, and Jefferson Hall hotels were among his places of residence.

For three months in 1966 he was a law partner of Peter Barbara in the Penobscot Building. He was so busy with clients in Lower Michigan that he missed two Thanksgivings with his family, in 1967 and 1968. He was still a legal resident of the 98th judicial district, and ran unsuccessfully on slips for district judge in the November 1968 election, losing 467 to 9,305.

Ted met some interesting and sometimes shady characters while he was practicing in Detroit. A man named Peter Lazaros, described as "a reputed Mafia informer," was indicted in 1967, along with James Hudnut—one of the principals of the law firm—on fraud charges, but never tried. Ted served as Lazaros's attorney at one time. In 1969 Lazaros was convicted of twelve counts of perjury after charging that a prosecutor had been paid bribes. During the trial Ted represented a man called Boo Boo Davis who testified that Lazaros' bribery claims were lies.

Lazaros appealed and the conviction was upheld in 1973. Sometime after leaving prison, in 1977, Lazaros stayed in a hotel somewhere and called a jeweler to bring in an assortment of gemstones for him to look over. He liked a certain four-carat diamond ring so much that he decided to swallow it. The $35,000 ring was discovered the following year when an autopsy was being performed on his body.[7]

Ted had numerous friends and clients in Lower Michigan. Sometime during the early 1960s he had met Daniel Zahari, a Dearborn fireman who was dismissed from his job after filing to run in the 1961 mayorial election against longtime incumbent Orville Hubbard.

The city discharged Zahari as soon as he filed his nominating petitions. Zahari had frequently criticized the mayor during his fifteen year career. He jokingly told a reporter from the *Detroit News* that he "might retain Hubbard as a play supervisor at Camp Dearborn. He deserves a quiet old age." His wife, he said, encouraged him to run for office, and her ownership of a tavern made his run possible, he told the newspaper. Zahari, who later became one of Ted's clients, fought a long battle in the courts in an attempt to be reinstated to the fire department.

---

[7] Ted Albert sued Peter Lazaros in Oakland County, Michigan on February 27, 1969 for slander or libel. "Peter E. Lazaros, by circulated affidavit charged that he gave me a $2,500 cashier's check to bribe Chief Judge Lesinski of the Court of Appeals." Ted represented Boo Boo Davis, who had earlier been sentenced to prison time for an extortion conviction and was then in the Wayne County jail awaiting trial on a "federal matter."

6

TRIBULATIONS

The practice of law can be a very thankless profession. Lawyers are often ranked far down on the list of respected professionals, alongside used car dealers and politicians. Sometimes when a lawyer wins a case for a client, the lawyer is resented for the fees he collects; if he loses a case or fails to obtain the results a client had in mind, he is good for nothing.

A former legal secretary recalled:

Mr. Albert had quite a following among area residents, apparently as a result of his years as prosecuting attorney. He took genuine interest in righting wrongs done to the average person and appeared to be more interested in seeking justice for them than in receiving compensation.

He joked about all of the payments he had received in produce, dairy and poultry over the years, but it didn't deter him. During my time in the office, he continued to help people with little means with as much enthusiasm as he would a major case against a corporate giant.

Ted's enthusiasm is further documented by a fellow lawyer who recalled how Ted would frequently walk into courtrooms carrying fifty pounds of lawbooks, and lay them out on the table.

The year 1970 was a sort of watershed in Ted Albert's career. During this decade Ted ran for office every few years and constantly battled with the State Bar Grievance Board who came at him with a veritable avalanche of complaints, all or most of which originated from his practice in Lower Michigan, and which seriously affected his candidacies and his law practice.

By the mid-70s Ted was hard at work on his promotion of the U.P. as the 51st state of Superior, perhaps in part because of disgust and contempt for the people in Lower

Michigan that he felt were harassing him. He never gave up or made concessions during that time.

In the summer of 1970 Ted announced his candidacy for judge of the 98th District, serving Gogebic and Ontonagon counties. He filed papers to run in the August primary; his opponent that fall, republican Eugene Zinn, had been appointed judge following the death in office of William S. Baird. Just before the election the Gogebic/Ontonagon Labor Council AFL/CIO ran an ad supporting Ted's candidacy.

In August 1970 Ted lost his appeal to the State Supreme Court on contempt charges stemming from the Fittante, Pitts and Dogans cases. A testimonial dinner was planned in his behalf and scheduled for the evening of October 17, 1970, but the local newspaper reported nothing about it. About one week before the election, the *Daily Globe* published an article:

High Court Upholds Ruling

A contempt of court conviction against a former Ironwood attorney was recently upheld by the Michigan Supreme Court.

Theodore Albert, who now resides in the Iron River area had been declared guilty of contempt of court for his failure, on three occasions, to take timely action when ordered by the Court of Appeals.

Albert, according to Michigan Reports (Vol. 383), was charged with the responsibility of perfecting his client's appeal in the Court of Appeals and was given additional time to act, after a delay of almost three years, and still failed to take "timely action."

Albert appealed the Court of Appeals decision to the Michigan Supreme Court but on Aug. 19, the Supreme Court upheld the conviction.

Albert asserted the contempt procedure must include a show-cause order based on an affidavit supporting the charged facts and also asserted the court could not institute such a proceeding on its own motion without becoming so personally interested as to be disqualified...

...Albert is a candidate for 98 District Judge of Gogebic and Ontonagon counties, in the Nov. 3 election.

Ted wrote a long letter to the *Daily Globe*, saying that the report was "locally conceived, not based on the facts," and

...intended to deceive all who would read it and particularly the voters of Gogebic and Ontonagon counties. The bare reading of the article would cause the reader to believe that there was currently some punishment to be yet exacted by the court.

It did not mention that some 56 or more lawyers were involved in the enforcement of the court's policy. That although the other attorneys were willing to pay the fines and the costs, yours truly challenged the legality of such costs contending that the legislature had not legislated such costs and the Supreme Court contemplated no such assessment. It was pointed out in my brief that the proceedings were initiated by the court and no person represented by me had made any complaint or was otherwise aggrieved.

It was also pointed out that the court did not initiate petitions for such proceedings as that would constitute the practice of law which the court is by law prohibited from doing. It would have been easy to pay the costs and forget about it but consistent with my usual conduct to challenge where challenge is necessary I proceeded with the blessings of all of the attorneys to bring this issue to light. It was a matter of interest to the legal profession.

I had prepared my case to ultimately be reviewed by the United States Supreme Court. The only issue before the court, in effect, was the legality of such costs. I was before the court not for contumacious conduct in the court but for my failure to pay the costs which I deemed illegal.

As Supreme Court Justice Kavanagh says in my paid political advertisement appearing today in this newspaper there was no involvement of my ability and my integrity and there should be none. It is my firm belief that the court respected my willingness to take issue in this matter. I have not appealed the decision of the court but the matter has been disposed of as adjudicated.

The reference to my candidacy for District Judge was wholly irrelevant to the news item and seemingly it was intended and it can be construed that I was not worthy of seeking judicial office. The Ironwood Daily Globe could have checked the story with me for background facts and to further make it a full story about the disposition of the matter. The failure to do so indicates the lack of desire to do so. It lends further to the conclusion that the intent was to injure and to cause detrimental effect on my election.

This statement is made following conversations had with the publisher and with the attorney for The Ironwood Daily Globe.

Ted lost the election to Judge Eugene Zinn, 8,376 to 3,158.

On January 20, 1971 Ted Albert filed a lawsuit against the *Ironwood Daily Globe*, and Elmer Tryon, its editor, asking for $350,000 in general damages because of his injured reputation and good standing in his profession; $500,

000 in special damages because the negative publicity affected his candidacy and "esteem of other attorneys, public authority and the judiciary;" and $350,000 in punitive damages "because the wilful and malicious publication" entitled him to "recover exemplary or punitive damages." Ted claimed "loss of earnings as Judge for a period of 17 years to age of 70, calculated at $25,000 per year."[8]

The *Daily Globe* was represented by lawyers Charles M. Humphrey, Jr. and Lawrence Weis, who, on February 8, 1971, filed a fifteen-page interrogatory consisting of 45 detailed questions for Ted to answer, virtually asking for his life's story. Ted filed his first response on April 26, 1971, coyly answering many of the interrogatories with the statement, "Requires no answer. Inadmissible under Rules of Evidence. [302.2(1)]." In May 1972 the court required him to answer those questions, and he filed a second answer on July 5, 1972.

---

[8] Gogebic County Court File 71-5, Theodore G. Albert, Plaintiff, vs Globe Publishing Company, a Michigan corporation, d/b/a Ironwood Daily Globe; Elmer Tryon, Jointly & Severally, Defendants.

In his reply Ted said that 75 persons questioned him about the *Daily Globe* article of October 28, 1970 and wanted to know if "there was a conviction, and if the same would not disqualify" him from holding office.

Ted was a very busy man at that time because he and several of his siblings were involved in a lawsuit concerning their father. Five of George Albert's children were suing two others. Ted was serving as attorney for four of his siblings in the lawsuit, filed on March 2, 1970. Albert had suffered a stroke in February 1969, and there was a family dispute over his care and the disposition of his property. Albert died during the time the suit was in progress, but Ted had removed himself from the case just a few weeks before. The remaining plaintiffs dropped the lawsuit one year later.

And so, in the midst of all of the other lawsuits that were tying him down, the State Bar Grievance Board came to him with a "Formal Complaint" on January 27, 1971, opening up a long legal battle that would last until 1979!

Among other things, a woman from Warren complained of giving Ted $100 to pursue a lawsuit against a nursing home where her mother had been staying, and had only been able to meet with him twice.

A man from Lansing complained of paying Ted an advance of $1,200 on a contingent fee agreement for handling a civil rights lawsuit against the city, claiming that Ted did not handle the case professionally.

A man from Redford Township was being sued by his credit union and Ted was to represent him. He said Ted failed to show up the court and the judge fined him $25.

A woman from Saginaw claimed she had engaged Ted to represent her in a lawsuit, paying him $250 for depositions, but could not get in touch with him later.

The "Formal Complaint" was signed by Richard Senter, Richard Kramer, and Louis Rosenzweig, of the Michigan State Bar Grievance Board. These complaints dated back to as early as 1967, with most dating from 1970, and Ted had already prepared and mailed in his replies. Many of the complaints stemmed from his having allegedly referred cases to a fellow attorney named Gus Cifelli who had an office across the hall from him in the Penobscot Building. Ted claimed Cifelli had promised to take care of various cases after Ted closed his office and returned to the U.P.[9]

In the case of the man from Lansing, Ted wrote a two-and-one-half page response in May 1970. He said the man's complaint was "replete with lies." The man had retained Ted on a contingent basis of 50%. A preliminary hearing ruled against him. 'Mr. X' complained, "Albert was going to appeal ... but because of another case he was working on I would have to remain patient."

A ten-day grace period expired without action, and the man's appeal was denied. In January 1970 'Mr. X' sued the city of Lansing and "paid Mr. Albert in full for his service, he did not appear at the hearing and thereby caused a warrant of arrest to be issued against me." He alleged he had paid Ted $1,200 "for costs in connection with the preparation and handling" of the case, but Ted said this was a lie.

Ted said he undertook this case "only after considerable discussion... relative to the facts as they applied to the existing law... that only under the most limited circumstances was there any law, from case precedent, that would find the defendant, city of Lansing, a 'person' as contemplated under the Civil Rights Act... "I told Mr. [X] that I would not be an insurer of the result in this type of case. I also made it clear that his insistence to have me represent him would have its drawbacks such as the expense of travel, lodgings and other expenses."

---

[9] The Club Chicaugon, located on Iron County Road 424, southeast of Iron River, Michigan, was incorporated under the name A & C Promotions. It was a popular resort for snowmobilers, wedding reception parties, and diners. Cifelli was a partner in the business.

Later Ted defended 'Mr. X' on gambling charges. "The work performed by me prior, during and after the preliminary examination, and in the circuit court is nothing for an attorney to be ashamed of. With respect to his complaint in that matter I did not receive notice of the arraignment." Ted was forced to reconsider the duty of representing 'Mr. X' due to "some unusual conduct... One such incident was a terrifying threat" 'Mr. X' made to Mrs. Albert that he would "send some people to the Upper Peninsula to kill" her and Ted!

Ted told the Grievance Board, "I will never be able to defend ['Mr. X'] and I hesitate to relate incidents, any more than is absolutely necessary. ['Mr. X'] is indebted to me. I shall bill him accordingly and in doing so, in as detailed a form as my time, my advice and my services warrant."

Many hearings were held in Lower Michigan before the State Bar. At first Ted was represented by a young lawyer named Roy Delaney, a partner of Armand Bove. In April 1971 Delaney requested an adjournment of the hearing due to Ted's pending litigation against the *Ironwood Daily Globe*. Delaney was later replaced by William J. McBrearty, who told the panel in December 1971 that the file on the 'Mr. X' case alone "must weigh fifteen pounds and represents work by Mr. Albert."

The Grievance Board suspended Ted's license to practice law for one year and fined him $1,183.88 in February 1972. In its report it claimed, "It is evident from the testimony Respondent is an itinerant lawyer who practices law out of a suitcase from motel and hotel rooms and not from a permanent office... Once having been retained it is virtually impossible to reach him..."

Ted took great offense at the Grievance Board's finding and continued a long process of filing motions and appeals. As of June 29, 1972, Ted was to be under a one-year suspension from the Bar. He went before the Michigan Supreme Court in July 1972, whose justices included his old nemesis G. Mennen Williams and John B. Swainson. The Court granted him a "stay of order of discipline." About this time Mr. X changed his story and claimed he had given Ted not $1,200 but $3,000 to $4,000.

Several of the complaints stated that the people who had hired Ted had a very difficult time getting in touch with him. One wrote that she was told "twenty people were desperately calling" his office; he told the Grievance Board, "That I can't deny. The usual day has more." He told them that his name was "in the phone books and yellow pages."

By the spring of 1972 Ted was considering another run for prosecuting attorney just to show everybody that he was still capable of practicing law even though the one-year suspension was hanging over him; all he would have needed was an assistant to take over certain duties. In one of the papers filed in his case he said he maintained "in his office in excess of 100 criminal and civil matters requiring attendance."

In March 1973 Ted was once again before the Michigan Supreme Court pressing an appeal of his suspension and fine. The court said, "Upon examining the briefs and the record and after hearing counsel for the parties, the Court is left with the impression that there may have been a failure to provide respondent with an adequate opportunity to defend the charges against him." The court remanded his case back to the Grievance Board.

Between 1971 and 1972 there were at least six articles about Ted's Grievance Board troubles published in the *Daily Globe*. Stories went around about Ted being "run out of Detroit." He claimed Elmer Tryon, editor of the *Daily Globe*, had told him sometime prior to publication of the offending October 1970 article, "in the presence of others that 'if the kikes don't get you the *Ironwood Daily Globe* will.' " Judge Zinn asked Tryon for help in defeating him, and Tryon told Ted, "We can't take the chestnuts out of the fire for you." A summary judgment in favor of the defendants was entered in Ted's lawsuit against the newspaper in February 1973.

In March 1974 the Grievance Board issued an Order of Discipline, wherein Ted was suspended from the practice of law for one year effective February 21, 1974, with a second one-year suspension following from February 21, 1975. He then filed a million-dollar lawsuit against the Bar of Michigan naming fifteen members, as well as Governor Milliken and the seven justices of the State Supreme Court. He claimed the defendants had "conspired to ruin his legal practice, libeled him and violated his constitutional rights... The defendants," he said, undertook "frantic efforts... to close plaintiff's business," and harrassed him. Ten more complaints had been filed against him since his hearing began in 1971 "because of unwarranted publicity."

In his papers he stated that he had twenty-one cases scattered over several counties that required his immediate attention. He said he "was severely damaged and irreparably injured in his reputation and his standing in the profession; that he has lost good and well meaning clients, who because of the terribly unfavorably designed publicity, have discharged movant from their service; others equally well meaning are seriously concerned about the continuation of deponent's legal services." The lawsuit was dismissed in October 1974.

Hearings before the Grievance Board and appeals continued for the following three years. In 1974 the *Pick & Axe*, published in Bessemer, Michigan by Mike Cowdery, described Ted as "a hot shot civil liberties attorney whose council is sought across the country. Ted is probably most well known for his efforts to establish the Upper Peninsula as the Fifty-first state. And that idea is not as screw ball as it might seem at first. It is legally possible and would serve to bring our government a lot closer to home. It would also give us direct representation in the Senate of the United States as well as in the House."

In late February 1976 Ted and the Grievance Board agreed to dismiss his appeal. He paid filing fees and costs to the Bar in May, and a hearing was held in September for his reinstatement to the Bar. An investigator went around the state interviewing people who knew or were acquainted with him. Some of the remarks the man collected were not complimentary. Ted's petition for reinstatement was denied in February 1977. So he began another round of motions and appeals which ended in the State Supreme Court.

In an interview published in the *Duluth News Tribune* in May 1978, when Ted was running for representative to the United States Congress, he called the Grievance Board cases "trumped up charges... All the charges were created by the bar. They even solicited grievances from a former client of mine." The article said Ted discounted "the charges, speaking darkly of large conspiracies."

I know too much.

Why should I repent for something I didn't do? I haven't done anything to hurt my campaign or anything to be ashamed of. I'm like the white driven snow compared to those bastards.

A woman cleaning my office put my shingle in the window without my knowledge, and my name was accidentally listed in the telephone directory with "attorney" after it. The Bar investigator who came up here to collect evidence for my reinstatement hearing only talked to my enemies.[10]

I have knowledge of past election tampering; criminal activity took place in regard to the 1964 election, which I intend to disclose in the future.

Most of my troubles stem from the 1953 Circuit Court election when I ran against Thomas Landers. He was a very popular judge. There was also a lot of turmoil with that Grand View Hospital case. It became evident to my friends that I was gushing against the wind.

---

[10] "Albert Theodore G. atty" appears in Ironwood telephone directories from 1972 to 1978; in the 1978-79 directory the "atty" was dropped; his name disappears in 1981-82; Ted said, "The cleaning woman put my sign in the window not knowing that there was a problem, and I did not know it since I was campaigning. Some insidious attorney made some points with Senter by reporting it. The FBI agent who investigated me for reinstatement was a team partner of Senter on the [Bar] task force."

It used to take me twenty-five minutes to walk two blocks in Ironwood because I was so popular; I can hardly believe I've lost my popularity. I can't understand, when the most popular person was Ted Albert... I can't understand how it could deteriorate so much. I don't intend for that to happen with this election. The Federal election commissioners will be right here watching.

As soon as I am sworn in I intend to propose enabling legislation to make the U.P. the fifty-first state.

Early in the fall of 1978 the Supreme Court, following almost one year of deliberation, ruled in Ted's favor. It said the "Bar could not require a suspended attorney to show remorse for an allegation for which he professes innocence... Any suspension must carry with it the conditions for reinstatement at the time that a suspension is handed down."

The *Nonesuch News* published in White Pine, Michigan, reported on and quoted parts of the decision:

Albert, who represented himself before the court, has done a great service to the individual members of the legal profession by forcing the rewriting of the rules under which the State Bar Association operates.

Albert had earlier succeeded in obtaining a U. S. Supreme Court ruling that there was no evidence of wrongdoing on his part which would warrant disbarment.... either directly or indirectly.

Ted had one more hurdle to cross. The Grievance Board charged he had "held himself out as a licensed practitioner" during his suspension. Furthermore, in order to return to practice, they claimed, he had to be recertified. The case went to the Michigan Supreme Court, and it decided on April 26, 1979 that there was no evidence to support the first claim, and because Ted's "status of suspension did not result from an actual Order of Suspension of three years or more... recertification was not applicable."

Gus Cifelli wrote to Ted, telling him, "It is difficult to imagine the suffering you have experienced these last few years... Our profession is getting back a man of outstanding...

extraordinary ability. It is a shame that it has taken so long to do so."

The Gogebic County Courthouse, built in 1887.

7

THE CANDIDATE

Ted Albert continued his struggle to gain election to public office, running for United States Representative in 1974 and 1978, and Senator in 1976. At the same time that he was attempting to gain political office he was also continuing his legal practice.

In January 1974 Ted accepted an invitation to sit on a panel discussing pornography at a college in the Lansing area, where he had a law office at the time. The college thanked him, saying, "Your extensive research and familiarity with the issue ... made you an excellent resource person... You really set the students thinking."

One year earlier an FBI agent and two other government people purchased tickets and watched a movie called *Deep Throat* at Cinema X Theater in Newport, Kentucky. It was the beginning of an investigation that led to a trial of several defendants on nine counts. American News Company, Inc., also known as American News Distributing Company, was found guilty of interstate transportation of pornography and fined $5,000. Ted served as their attorney when the case went to the United States Court of Appeals, 6th District, where a decision was made in July 1975.

In 1974 Ted became involved in the Michigan Human Rights Party, a radical, socialist party formed in the early 1970s by left-wing students and activists from southern Lower Michigan. The party emblem was the hippopotamus, a creature best suited to life in rivers, and dangerous to any other creature that should happen to approach it, lest the hippo should bite them in half.

Ted said the HRP had "new and refreshing appeal. More than at any other time in history an independent party has the opportunity to bring itself to the public. The two old parties are starting to look like crabs in a box. You can't tell them apart."

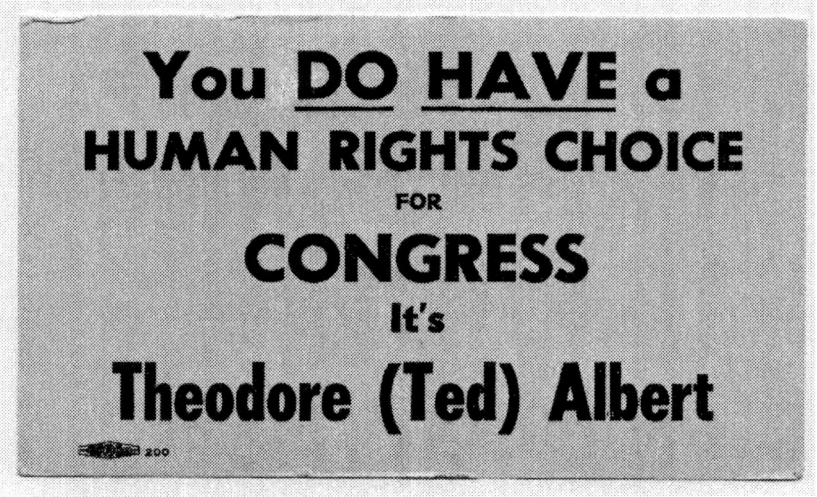

In one newspaper interview he said, "If elected, my first order of business would be to take care of the matters of conscience. Such issues as amnesty, the problems of aging, and women's rights deserve top priority and immediate action."

Ted, as a result of having a law office in Lansing, was probably acquainted with Zolton Ferency, a Lansing lawyer, professor and former democrat, who was active in the party and ran as its gubernatorial candidate. Ted's association with this political party may have been either a marriage of convenience and / or possibly a way of thumbing his nose in the faces of his detractors while gaining a platform for his 51st state of Superior movement; Matt Laitala of the Michigan DNR had already referred to Project Seafarer opponents as "a bunch of damn commies."

In May of 1974 Ted accepted the party's nomination for candidate to Congress, and issued a news release, stating in part,

The people of the 11th district, as elsewhere are now aware that the old political parties ignore the needs of the many and their respective conduct indicates a failure to respond to the social, economic, and political needs of the people. The old parties have continued the movement widening the separation of the government from the people, a situation the concerned citizen deems intolerable since the power of government belongs to the people it governs. This is the time for change. The 11th district needs a representative who is dedicated to evolving new human programs which nuture the creative worth and dignity of the individual, and which reflect the needs of our society.

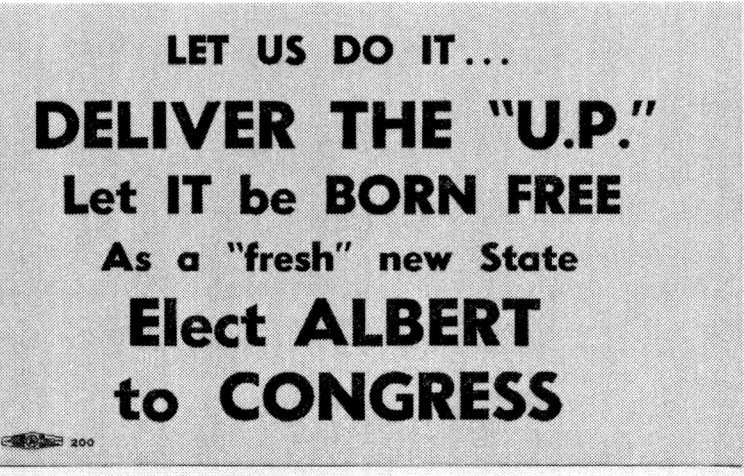

Mike Cowdery, editor of the Bessemer *Pick & Axe*, reported on Ted's candidacy, stating, "Most folks hereabouts have heard of Ted Albert. He's a controversial character—that's a fact." Ted spent $300 on his campaign, spending $150 for ads in the *Pick & Axe* and another $150 on campaign cards. He reported $300 in donations to his campaign, raised from a brother and a relative. When the election was held in November, Ted received only 34 votes in Gogebic County, and only 2/10th of one per-cent of the total vote cast in the district!

His law career continued, and he farmed out his services to corporations, preparing various legal papers and documents from his office in Ironwood for corporate clients. He told a newspaper reporter in 1978, "I have done a job in sustaining myself the last few years. I have suffered, but I have not brown nosed or knuckled." In 1974 Ted formed the U.P. 51st State of Superior, Inc. to promote his independence movement for the U.P.

The would-be senator.

In 1976 he again ran on the Human Rights Party ticket, this time for United States Senator. The Committee to Elect Theodore G. Albert U.S. Senator was based in Flint, Michigan. Envelopes and letterheads were printed for his campaign, and he talked the HRP into adopting his statehood proposal as part of its platform.

In June of 1976 he said he "was working almost alone" to create the 51st state "because if this thing should fall flat on its face, I [do] not want to embarrass a considerable membership... I hardly stand a chance of being elected unless lightning should strike." Once again, he received only 2/10th of one per cent of the vote cast.

In the spring of 1978 another election loomed over the U.P., and Ted was getting ready for another contest, perhaps his last major campaign. In January he announced he was running for Congress on the democratic ticket. He had been in touch with his old friend Frank Hook, by then an elderly man. Hook wrote a letter to an acquaintance who was high up in the hierarchy of the AFL-CIO, asking for union support of Ted's candidacy. Hook's contact replied, "I have checked with our people in Michigan and, very frankly, they do not have a very high opinion of your friend, Theodore G. Albert. I am afraid there is no way anybody can persuade them to back him in the race for Congress."

Ted issued another press release in February, stating,

My ongoing promotional activity, of long duration toward making the Upper Peninsula the 51st State has made me aware, in a realistic manner, of the issues requiring attention and study. This is, especially, true as it relates to the issues of economic salvation, independence and security. All of such concerns are equally applicable to the 12 northernmost counties of the Lower Peninsula belonging to our District. It should be common knowledge that I have spent the last four years devoting my time to writing and talking about our welfare and our interests. I have, proudly, broadcast and otherwise publicized our existence and our hopes in the national, state and district news media. Such publications have created for us a national identity, recognition and interest in our area and in our cause. I have, without abatement, proudly exhibited and promoted our area as the provisional Governor of the State of Superior and as a sincere and vocal Ambassador of Northern Michigan. In a tangible way, it can be said that I have had some success in creating a new interest and a new posture and newly discovered national and state identity. Whenever and wherever the opportunity availed itself, I have spread the word of the abundance of our natural and human resources.

Likewise, I have had a degree of success in convincing others of our native, frontiersmen-like spirit and a national recognition of the high average of the intelligence and literacy of the people who comprise our district.

Likewise, I did not find it difficult to extol and otherwise brag about the work skills and aptitudes of our people. By reason of the energy shown in promotional activity, our program of hopes and goals has been placed before the President of the United States, in detailed and total input and at his request. It will not be injurious to our betterment, if and when insistence results in a personal interview and discussion with the President as is contemplated. All of this was done without the leverage or influence of public office or political motivation.

Our old problems will remain current and unresolved and newly created problems will obtain the same result unless we dedicate ourselves to rid the prevailing apathy to progress through new and innovative programs and ideas. Unless the highest degree of communication and exchange of ideas is made possible, we may cement and fix the dangerous belief that nothing can be done in our district to alleviate a postured, stagnant status quo.

The *Duluth News Tribune* called him "Tempestuous Ted." He told a reporter, "My dad always said if you waiver from your convictions, if you can't do the job right, come on up and sell neckties. I decided long ago I never wanted to sell neckties. I've always had a propensity for and an inclination toward public service... Between 1946 and 1956 was the height of my popularity; there wasn't anyone who doubted that I'd end up as a United States senator."

Ted's political philosophy and beliefs were somewhat antithetical to those of the Human Rights Party. In his *News*

Tribune interview he stated that if the U.P. were an independent state he planned "to cut the size of our government to cut costs. The ideal government would be no government at all. I would cut the 259 Michigan state agencies down to 30 for the State of Superior; we don't need a cherry commission up here. The state of Michigan has 498 judges; the State of Superior would only need about one for each county."

Ted publicized his ideas on controlling inflation in a series of articles submitted to the *Daily Mining Gazette* in Houghton, Michigan in May 1978, which boiled down to four main points. "We certainly tried the gamut of controls—one economic control after another... The four-point plan giving the free enterprise system a chance is as follows:

"1. Balance the federal budget as quickly as possible.
"2. Increase incentives to save; the first $1,000 of interest earned on savings accounts should be tax-free.
"3. Increase incentive to invest through tax deferments.
"4. Do not stimulate housing by more government intervention."

He felt there was another problem; "Government seized absolute control over the supply of money... dollars are no longer pieces of gold metal but are pieces of paper... They print as much money as they want—as much as they can get away with... essentially legalized counterfeiting... The Federal Reserve System should be abolished," he said, and "the country should return to the gold standard." Ted found his inspiration on this topic by reading *What Has Government Done to Our Money?*, by Murray N. Rothbard.

A testimonial dinner was held in his honor at the V.F.W. Hall in Mass City in late May of 1978. Frank Hook attended, telling the audience, "I will stump the 11th District forcefully proclaiming my endorsement of Ted Albert... I praise God for the privilege of endorsing a man of such high moral character and steadfast devotion to justice and truth!"

Ted was a vociferous opponent of the United States Navy's 'Project Sanguine,' also known as 'Seafarer' or 'Elf,' an underground grid that would have broadcast 'extremely low frequency' (elf) signals to submarines in the event of a nuclear war; it was a sort of doomsday project. The Laurentian Shield that underlies much of the U.P. was thought to provide an ideal natural transmitter. Many Yoopers resented the idea of being placed into a potential nuclear bullseye after the project had been chased out of other states. Ted opposed the project throughout the 1970s and advocated a referendum in the U.P. to settle the question.

Ted advocated the construction of a north-south canal from Lake Superior to Lake Michigan, beginning at either Munising or AuTrain and ending at Manistique or Little Bay De Noc. He felt such a canal "would bring world trade to our doors," as well as reducing traffic at the Soo Locks, while providing cheap hydroelectric power and an unlimited water supply.

He was in favor of voter initiatives whereby citizens could vote on issues if they disagreed with the way an issue was handled by Congress. Petitions would be circulated to secure the required number of signatures, and an issue would be put to popular vote. "I don't think our United States Congress is so sacred that it should have a monopoly over law making... The deliberations of Congress are increasingly dominated by special interests. The average American has little to say over most issues."

Ted wanted the U.P.'s natural resources to be turned into manufactured goods in the U.P. instead of being exported. He felt that was a way of creating jobs for local citizens. The U.P., he said, suffered from a "trade deficit," exporting about $32,000,000 a year in raw materials and importing the finished goods.

He told the National Right To Work Committee that workers should not be forced to join unions against their will—union membership should not be compulsory. He was opposed to abortion and gun control, and supported smaller government and a smaller federal budget.

In late June of 1978 G. Mennen Williams paid a visit to Mass City, where, as one newspaper said, "Ted Albert, candidate for Congress, his long time friend, had invited him on behalf of the Citizens Committee for Better Government, Inc." Only a month earlier Ted had told a newspaper reporter that he considered himself the "alter ego of G. Mennen Williams." Thus Williams, who had been denounced as a stooge of Big Labor back in 1958, was once again a friend; Williams sat on the Michigan Supreme Court, which was preparing to reach a decision on Ted's long-fought case against the State Bar!

Armand Cirilli wrote in the *Iron County Miner*, published in Hurley, Wisconsin —Ironwood's sister city—that "Ted is not dull... you sure n hell would know that he was there," if he were elected. Just a few days before the primary, Ted appeared on WNMU TV broadcast from Northern Michigan University in Marquette. When the primary took place he lost to Keith McLeod of Marquette, 11,369 to 4,936.

On August 21, 1978 Ted announced his write-in candidacy:

The decision I have made to involve myself in the November General Election is not a hasty or an ill-considered one. I know, perhaps, better than anyone else that seldom is such a race considered and seldom is it won. I know too, that it will be a Herculean task to contact all of the voters and to inform them on the procedures necessary to cast their votes. It will be difficult but it can and will be done. Citizens who are expected to learn and apply the metre and litre measures intended, insanely, to be imposed upon us will find it less difficult to register or write-in votes on paper or machine ballots. It will require and I will demand that State and County election commissions cooperate to the fullest legal extent in making provisions for an adequate supply of paper ballots and additionally, for the educational process the voting public is entitled to. This type of candidacy is provided by law. I am, simply, engaging in my legal entitlement and my rights as a U. S. citizen under the law. By undertaking this challenge, I do not trespass upon, violate or interfere with anyone else's rights. My candidacy is derived from independent judgment, aided only by the strong and convincing will and desire of my many friends and supporters.

In the primary I pointed out that the party hierarchy was pulling strings and not intending to permit an open and free primary. They pulled so many strings that in their confusion the nominee, who landed on his feet on their stage, was not the one they really wanted... and was not one of them... or truly representative of the Democratic party. Now, in typical hypocritical fashion, they will gather around mouthing words to show a reluctant willingness to cooperate and make their efforts cohesive. I would not be true to myself—and I would do violence to my better judgment if I would partake in such tongue-in-cheek promotion.

I am not about to spoil a Democratic victory in November. I intend, however, to provide an opportunity for a real one. I am of the firm opinion that I will be providing a choice of a real Democrat to vote for where none, now, exists. As a Democrat, I am not concerned about the anticipated havoc, denunciations and aspersions. I am immune. The so-called, dictatorial "regulars" should have anticipated a day of reckoning.

The *Pick & Axe* reported, Ted "has found new strength after losing the Democratic nomination... speaking of the issue of metric measurement, Albert termed their use 'unwise if not downright Un-American.' " Then, two months later, another report appeared in the *Pick & Axe*: "With a sad smile and a tearful eye, Ted Albert bowed out of the 11th district congressional race... Albert had won heavy support from this end of the peninsula in the Democratic primary, but lost the district wide nomination..."

Ted issued the final news release of his 1978 campaign, saying,

The decision to withdraw was preceded by a careful study of the difficult undertaking. I immediately began a careful study of all of the particular references and statutory and rule provisions for a write in paster, sticker and slip candidacy. What I had deemed to be possible is utterly impossible to accomplish without an expenditure of at least several hundred thousand dollars. I heard the voices of despair and the forecasts of futility. I felt that my sincere desire would only result in a heavy imposition of the special task of asking for a write in or slip vote from my many friends and supporters. It became perfectly clear that I could not accomplish the task...

Ted Albert endorsed Keith McLeod in no uncertain terms. "He is an honest man and I am satisfied beyond doubt that he is mentally equipped." George Gerovac of Marenisco told the *Pick & Axe*, "I would have liked to had Ted in Congress, but now that he's not running anymore, maybe he can get back to the business of making the U.P. a separate state."

The door to Ted Albert's office upstairs in the Albert Building, home of the U.P. 51st State of Superior, Inc.

8

THE POLITICS OF YOOPER SEPARATISM

By some point in the 1970s, people began referring to residents of the Upper Peninsula as "Yoopers." The word was phonetically derived from the abbreviation "UP'er." Something about the growth of big government and its increasing interference in local affairs and the lives of ordinary citizens had many Yoopers, as well as citizens of other regions and states, riled up by the middle of that decade. The phenomenon of big government played a role in fostering the rise of renewed interest in separate statehood for the U.P.

Ted's former legal secretary said,

The 51st State of Superior movement had already been established by the time I arrived in October 1972. He talked about it, but I wasn't involved in any of the activity at that time.

I do recall locals saying that we shouldn't become a state, that we should secede from the Union and become an independent *country* known as Superior. That way, the story goes, we would receive foreign aid and be paid to allow U. S. military installations to guard against polar missile attacks from the Russians. In addition, we would control the trade through entry into Lake Superior from the Soo locks, and develop our own minerals and expansive forests controlled by the state and federal governments! Folks were very angry about our double-digit unemployment rate at the time while watching millions of dollars go to third world countries.

A circle of supporters of Ted Albert's proposed State of Superior sprang up. In 1974 Benjamin F. Smith of Ada, Michigan, a student of "land economics," published chapters 1 and 15 from a manuscript he had spent years working on. His planned opus was to be called *The Prime Principle*, espousing his theories of land ownership and taxation. In the introduction to his publication, entitled *Latifundia in Gitche Gumee, A scientific study of despoilment of land and people in Michigan's Upper Peninsula*, he wrote,

Is it possible that there is a Land Cultural Directive which, in effect, says 'hear no evil,' 'see no evil,' and 'speak no evil' about the land tenure system that we follow?

Shouldn't we at least look at the cultural directive that tells us to grab all the land and natural resources we can and make a profit at the expense of our neighbors? Shouldn't we think about it before we condemn future generations to feudalism, exploitation, and poverty? Shouldn't we listen to the voices of history and science? I say we should. Won't you look, think, and listen with me?

Smith studied land ownership in the U.P. The U.P. consisted of 7,240,000 acres, 31.2 per cent of which was government land. Another 13.6 per cent was held by only six companies and was carried on the books as state-subsidized forest reserve land, taxed at greatly reduced rates.

Owners of mineral rights paid no real estate taxes at all (unless they also held the surface rights), and yet the vast untapped reserves of iron, copper, nickel, silver, and even gold, represented the U.P.'s highest claim to fame and past and future prosperity.

Smith believed that low assessments on mineral lands tended to encourage "owners to hold them idle until demand is more profitable." By taxing mineral rights, he contended, owners would feel more compelled to either develop mines or sell out to someone who would. Ted believed in this concept, and was well-aware of Smith's publication.

Smith proposed statehood for the U.P. as the state of Hiawatha:

The people of Michigan's U.P., perhaps more than those in any other part of the United States, have the spirit of '76. They are freedom-loving, two-fisted, brave, but perhaps too tolerant and long-suffering. Politically they might go for a land-tax state. They outnumber the large landowners thousands to one.

When the Great Depression struck in the 1930s, much of the real estate in the western U.P. was given up for taxes, and later bought up by the federal government to form the Ottawa National Forest, which eventually acquired close to a million acres.

In 1967 Roy Ahonen, a lumberman from Ironwood, protested the loss of forest land to the government as the Ottawa swallowed up more and more land:

> What can we expect under federal development? Instead of revenues we are faced with nothing but costs to the taxpayers. Initially there were acquisition costs of over $6,000,000 and the Forest Service estimates development costs in excess of $10,600,000 and annual operating costs of $437,700...
>
> The intensified development of Sylvania under private enterprise would have created a tremendous impact on the local economy in the way of direct payrolls and related services.

Ahonen and others believed that dedicating so much of our land to "wilderness" was a virtual guarantee of economic stagnation for the surrounding communities.[11]

Karl Magnuson, a former university professor, moved to Matchwood Township in Ontonagon County in 1972, settling in Topaz where he became a farmer. He was later elected clerk of Matchwood Township and became active in the Upper Peninsula Federation of Land Owners, formed in 1976 with headquarters in Ishpeming. He delivered a talk at a meeting in 1978, explaining why he became involved in the group, and attempting to explain his view of what was taking place in the country. His talk was printed in the organization's official publication, *The U.P. Landowner*:

> I had always considered myself to be a political person, but when I moved to the Upper Peninsula to become a farmer my thinking about politics underwent a radical transformation... I had come to view the purposes of our educational institutions with suspicion. But I had also begun to see a conflict between the actual conditions of my existence (as a state subsidized employee) and my notions about what a democratic society should be.

---

[11] *Ironwood Daily Globe*, October 11, 1967, page 9.

Magnuson became aware of a "land use plan" that was about to place "most of the countryside off-limits to development." These "land use plans" were "executed under the supervision of... the Western Upper Peninsula Planning and Development Region, or simply WUPPDR."

He pointed out that when local people opposed the 'development region' they were denounced as "right-wing fanatics and John Birchers;" when they spoke out about the U.S. Forest Service spraying chemical defoliants on 'junk trees' they were denounced as "enviromentalists;" when local citizens and the Bessemer *Pick & Axe* spoke up about Project Seafarer, "Matt Laitala, our Natural Resources Commissioner, called us communists... he has referred publically to Mike Cowdery's Pick & Axe... as the Bessemer Hammer & Sickle."

Magnuson said the real struggle of our time was not between left and right, but with another subtle process that was taking place; the hoopla about the struggle between right and left was "a diversionary tactic by those who possess and would seek control.... a smokescreen that obscures and diverts people's attention from a real and terrifying process that has developed, with frightening rapidity, in capitalist and socialist countries alike... as C. Wright Mills said, 'the enormous enlargement and the decisive centralization of all the means of power and decision... an enormous striving on the part of the very few for economic and political control over all the rest.' "[12]

In early July 1975 the U.P. 51st State of Superior, Inc. met at the Matchwood Township Hall, where Karl Magnuson spoke about Project Sanguine. The project, he felt, presented many dangers, both ecological and economic. If disputes arose between landowners and government, who would win?

Supporters of the State of Superior had another organization called Operation Action U.P. to stir up their passions. Operation Action U.P. was denounced as "a special interest

---

[12] *The U.P. Landowner*, June 1978, Vol. 3, No. 4.

group formed by Lower Peninsula businessmen." It was headquartered in Detroit and "widely known to represent large corporations, special interests, particularly moneyed interests." All of its officers except one were from the Lower Peninsula. The one exception pointed out by opponents was Raymond Smith, president of Michigan Technological University in Houghton. Smith, they claimed, "seemed to be hoping for a windfall of research money from the military... The very existence of a corporation having little or no tangible base in the U.P., yet claiming to speak on behalf of the economic interests of the U.P., should put all U.P. citizens on inquiry."

Magnuson made a motion for the U.P. 51st State of Superior, Inc. to issue a formal statement of opposition to Project Sanguine, and was seconded by Pat Kitzman. Ted's wife Dorothy duly recorded the minutes. The resulting resolution was sent to all units of goverment from local on up to the federal level, including President Jimmy Carter. The anti-Sanguine resolution was mailed on July 30, 1975.

Dominic Jacobetti was a democrat state representative from Negaunee and a supporter of separate statehood for the U.P. "We would have two U.S. senators representing 300,000 people. As it is, we've never had a U.S. senator from the U.P." Jacobetti had jumped aboard the statehood bandwagon and "named himself governor," thus prompting Ted to quip, "I hope the state bird craps on his head." Jacobetti remarked, "I don't even know he exists. He doesn't know what he's talking about. He's not progressive. He's regressive. He has no following and everything he touches turns sour. He would destroy the effort."[13]

Two years earlier, in 1975, a photo had appeared in the *Pick & Axe* showing Jacobetti pretending to sew a fifty-first star on the national flag. Ted could be seen in the background, behind Jacobetti's right shoulder. "GRANDSTANDER," the caption read; "State Rep. Dominic 'Jake' Jacobetti poses,

---

[13] Judith Yates Borger, "Michigan's Superior Notion," *Northliner Magazine*, Sept.-Oct. 1977, 17.

pretending to be sewing a symbolic fifty-first star on Old Glory, while Ted Albert, the real impetus behind the statehood movement, continues to work in the background. 'Somebody has to take care of the little domestic chores,' says Albert. 'Besides, it keeps them out of the way where the real work is being done.' "[14]

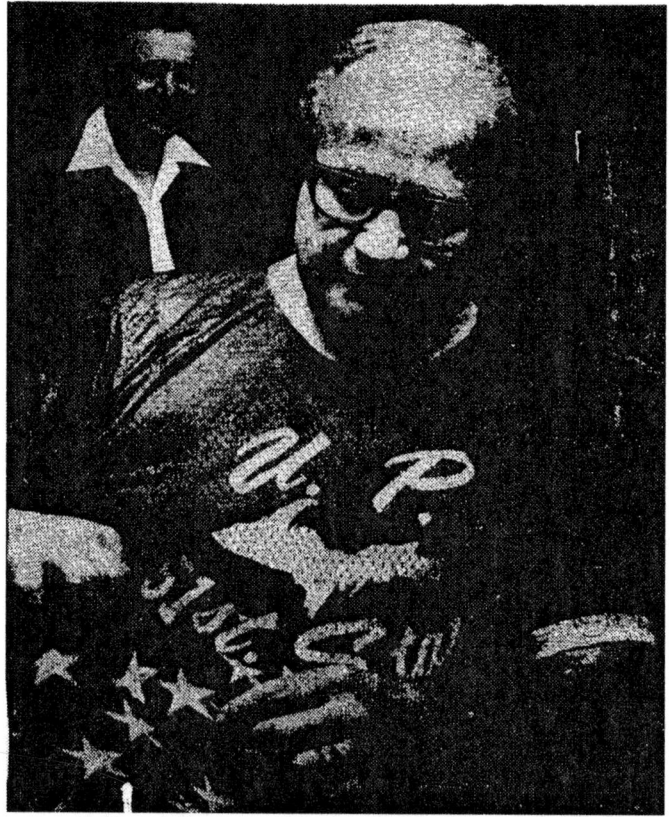

Ted Albert and Dominic Jacobetti, 1975.

By the beginning of 1975 Jacobetti and republican state senator Bob Davis of Gaylord requested a formal opin-

---

[14] The *Marquette Mining Journal* ran this same photo on the front page of its Saturday supplement on August 9, 1975, with Ted's picture blacked out!

ion from Michigan Attorney General Frank Kelley on the possibility of making the U.P. a separate state. "Whether or not the State of Superior will become a reality is up to the people who live there and the state legislature," he answered. Referenda were held later that year, but the results were disappointing; the few people who bothered to vote turned the idea down two to one. Ted later shrugged off the voting, blaming the poor showing on a lack of promotion prior to the referendum.

The Michigan legislature formed a special committee to study the feasibility of statehood for the U.P., and Jacobetti was a member; it never held a meeting. In September 1975 Ted sent a letter to Governor Milliken asking him to disband the committee. "It represents an unwarranted interference in our affairs... No one here has requested these hearings. No one in Lansing included us in on the creation of the committee."

The 1970s were also the heyday of state senator Joe Mack, another native of Ironwood. When Mack got into the trailer business in the early 1950s, Ted tried to do what he could to secure a steady supply of steel for Superior Steel Fabricating Co., writing a letter to the N.P.A.—an old federal government alphabet agency left over from the New Deal and World War Two era.

Mack's political career began in 1960 and lasted until 1986. His motto was "100% U.P.," and he was known for his loud plaid suitcoats. Sometimes he was known to wear a little tie clip shaped like the U.P., with a tiny mitten hanging off the end—a joke at the expense of the Lower Peninsula. Mack's picture appeared along with Jacobetti's on "Superior 51st State" tee shirts.

Disillusionment with state government spread out over the region by 1975, and in April of that year the commissioners of Vilas County, Wisconsin met at their courthouse. The "51st State Ad Hoc Committee" was called to order by Francis

Dussault, and Ray Klassen of Boulder Junction was elected chairman, with John Glaeser of Lincoln serving as secretary.

Ted addressed the group, and plans were made to meet with the Michigan U.P. 51st State of Superior, Inc. A resolution was adopted and published:

WHEREAS, the northern two thirds of Wisconsin is completely at the political and economic mercy of the southern one-third, and,

WHEREAS, this constitutes taxation without representation, and under the present one-man, one-vote concept, there can be no reversal of, nor relief from, the tyranny of power over justice, and,

WHEREAS, the northern sixteen counties of the State of Wisconsin, having the fewest people, and therefore the fewest votes, in the Wisconsin State Legislature, are the most vulnerable to this intolerable injustice, and,

WHEREAS, the Upper Peninsula of the State of Michigan, composed of fifteen counties and approximately 300,000 people, is in a comparably intolerable situation, and,

WHEREAS, the Upper Peninsula of Michigan is holding an advisory referendum in November 1975 to consider withdrawing from the Lower Peninsula and forming a new State of the United States, and,

WHEREAS, the Upper Peninsula of Michigan and the northern section of Wisconsin have a common boundary, common problems, common resources, and common goals,

NOW, THEREFORE, BE IT RESOLVED, that the Vilas County Board shall establish an ad hoc committee to explore the possibility of severing alliance with the State of Wisconsin and promoting the severing of the other fifteen northern counties from the state of Wisconsin with the stated purpose of joining with the Upper Peninsula of the State of Michigan in the formation of the 51st State of the United States of America.

Dated this 15th day of April, 1975

s/ Phillip A. Brandner   s/ E. C. Zimpelmann
s/ Arthur Brunetta   s/ Robert L. Croker Sr.

Vilas County was protesting "loss of local authority and state tax policies." Wisconsin state government favored the southeast part of the state. Former Congressman Alvin O'Konski of Wisconsin was in favor of the statehood idea, but warned the U.S. Senate was a formidable hurdle: "jealous of its rights and power and not likely to look with favor on a new state that would add two senators."

Thus was born the Northern Wisconsin 51st State of Superior, Inc., led by Thomas Forster of Presque Isle, Wisconsin, editor of the *Walleye Street Journal*. Ted offered his opinion, stating, "We're both the stepchildren of our capitals, the forgotten people of the lower part of the state[s]. I think the people in Wisconsin realize it may not be possible to join movement right now, but neither is hurting the other in trying to achieve statehood on its own. The more people that can be involved in this the better."

In September 1975 the two statehood groups announced the appointment of Laird Brooks Schmidt of Eagle River, Wisconsin as their public relations counsel. A joint rally was held at the Holiday Inn in Hurley, Wisconsin on October 25, 1975. The event was publicized with newspaper articles and posting of flyers around the area, but only about two dozen people showed up at the rally despite the fact that the two organizations claimed between 150 to 200 members each.

Some of Ted's ideas for supporting a new state were not entirely appreciated. He was pushing the idea of turning parts of the State of Superior into a "Monte Carlo" on the Great Lakes, using gambling to attract tourist dollars and tax revenues. He wanted to have a "new resident tax" that would force out-of-state settlers to pay more taxes. Some people doubted his claims of reducing government and were afraid that a welfare state was in the making, if for no other reason than that a new State of Superior would be hard pressed to support itself, or so some claimed.

A study by the Michigan legislature in 1973 claimed the U.P. paid $70 million in state taxes and received $100 million. It seems most of the larger landowners and taxpayers in the U.P. were skeptical of the idea of statehood. A gentleman who wrote a weekly business column in the *Marquette Mining Journal* looked into the tax situation about 1976 and reported he had found that Yoopers paid about $100 million a year in taxes. The annual spending for schools, hospitals, roads, and welfare would not be met, he claimed.

The U.P.'s colleges were also generally skeptical of the advantages of separate statehood. John Jamrich, president of Northern Michigan University, told a reporter, "I think [statehood] is legally possible. But my guess, based on a casual look at figures, is that it is probably not practical." He said the five U.P. colleges cost $37 million to operate in 1976.

Pat Kitzman of Matchwood Township, a member of the U.P. 51st State of Superior, Inc., ran for state representative in the democratic primary held in August 1978. He criticized the construction of "Taj Mahals" on U.P. college campuses "while reducing state aid formulas so that we can no longer afford to keep our neighborhood schools open. It's at the grade school level that we need to teach them to read, write, calculate, and love liberty." Kitzman decried Representative Rusty Hellman, Matt Laitala, crooked bureaucrats, and special interests.

"You wake up one morning and find out that some Wilderness Society hundreds of miles away has been admiring your property on a map and has nominated it for inclusion in a wilderness area," he said. Some made fun of Kitzman's rustic home in Matchwood Township, and he told them, "It isn't much of a house, but what's important is that it's a good home."

Kitzman was defeated in the primary, losing to Hellman, 5,130 to 3,983; not a bad showing for the man from Matchwood township.

His reward for speaking out and getting involved in politics came several days later. An anonymous caller tried to get him in trouble, telling the Social Security office in Ironwood that Kitzman had failed to report ownership of real es-

tate and an insurance settlement when he applied for SSI and disability in 1977. He was indicted in December 1979, tried in July 1980, and acquitted; he had sold the property in 1971 and received the insurance settlement several months after being denied benefits.

Before Ted's run for United States Congress in 1978, a group called the Citizen's Committee for Better Government, Inc. was organized in Mass City, Michigan. At least two of the people involved in its formation were friends of his: Melvin D. Peterson and Raymond Hardy; the former served as secretary of the "Committee To Elect Theodore G. Albert To Congress" later that year. Six people signed the "Creed of The Citizen's Committee" on January 4, 1978 stating its goals, which included fighting against...

...abuses by individuals who partake in the administration of government from township to the federal level... promot[ing] better government... evaluat[ing] candidates for elective and appointive offices, and with candor and fairness present our recommendations and our reasons for same to the People... We shall not be directed by individuals with selfish goals...

This country has engaged in too many conflicts, costly to life, limb, and our secured destinies to permit the abandonment or relinquishment of those very cherished and revered principles that people fought, died, and suffered for. To be blind to what is happening, to fail to recognize a growing deterioration of our government, and its true purposes, would be pure mockery and a sad commentary. This would prove the futility of our sacrifices abroad, while erosion has been permitted to grow at home to the extent that little, or nothing, is left of what we were told, and what we believed we were fighting for.

One can detect the hand of Ted Albert in the "Creed," and it is quite possible that he wrote it himself. He did not particularly care for President Jimmy Carter; when he ran for Congress in 1978 he voiced a low opinion of Carter's performance: his giveaway of the Panama Canal Zone, his welfare reform, and his entire cabinet.

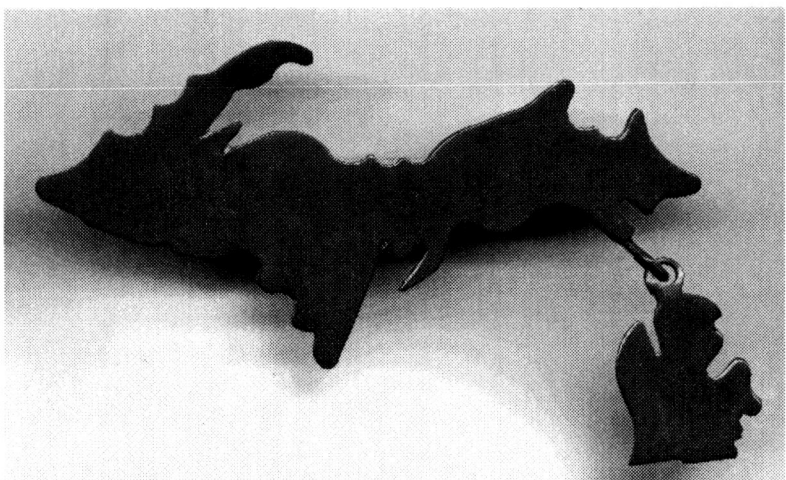

This homemade copper tie clip from the 1970s was a Yooper cultural statement.

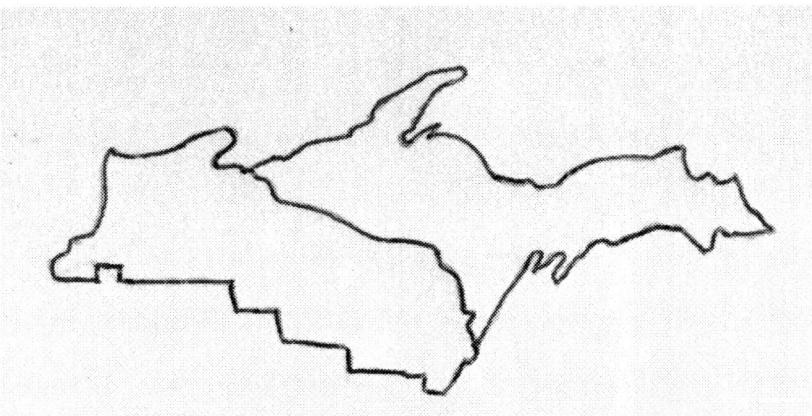

The State of Superior as envisioned if the northern counties of Wisconsin were united with the Upper Peninsula of Michigan. This version includes 17 Wisconsin counties, but anywhere from 16 to 21 were predicted to join the movement. The population of the two sections would be close to 1,000,000. There was also talk of including at least twelve counties from the Lower Peninsula of Michigan.

9

FIGHTING FOR SUPERIOR

It was sometime in February of 1974 that Ted sat down one day and began formulating his plans to push for Upper Peninsula statehood. With a yellow legal pad in front of him, he thought out a logical process of working toward statehood, and started scribbling notes on the pad.

He envisioned a corporate charter for the U.P. 51st State of Superior, Inc., along with articles of incorporation, an economic feasibility statement, declaration of intent, thesis, poem, and the famous divorce filing from 1959. He wrote down, "Mini model government— ideas —framework of ideas;" the attorney general's opinion was needed, and he had to compile a background bibliography, as well as prepare a sample statehood petition.

Ted dreamed up the idea of producing "Superior Border Patrol armbands," and came up with a design for a large poster. At the bottom of the page he wrote, "A statement of the conflict of our Constitutional provision between Art. IV Sec. 3."

Ted said he studied the reports of the Alaska Statehood Committee in order to gain an idea of what needed to be done. The free publicity somehow came to him, partly because of his constant political activity, and running for office on the Human Rights Party ticket in 1974-76.

Within a few years articles about Ted and his 51st state movement had appeared in *Grit* magazine, the *Bessemer Pick & Axe*, *Chicago Daily News*, *Chicago Daily Tribune*, *Detroit Free Press*, *Detroit News*, *Duluth News Tribune*, *Grand Rapids Press*, *Ironwood Daily Globe*, *Iron River Reporter*, *Lansing State Journal*, and *Marquette Mining Journal*, among others.

In March 1976 Ted was riled by a billboard he saw near Durand, Michigan advertising Ford automobiles. It carried a map of Michigan—but just the mitten, an all-too-common sight that always ticked off many Yoopers. He sat down and composed an audacious three-page letter to the Ford Motor Company, telling them in part,

The recent and much publicized, projected and displayed advertisement of the Ford Motor Company, depicting the State of Michigan as consisting, only, of the Lower Peninsula is, abhorrently, indicative of the shameless and impudent continuance of the evidence of the lack of communal regard or consideration of the Upper Peninsula.

In my assumed capacity as the de facto governor of the de facto State of Superior, I respectfully request that the Ford Motor Company voluntarily and gratuitously contribute to the promotion of the State of Superior by depositing in the name of this corporation, for its purpose and use, the sum of $50,000.00 in a bank of its choosing in each of the 15 counties of the U.P. Logic and reason dictate that such a sum is but a mere pittance when compared to the multi-million dollar, irrevocable advertising cost now entailed. Making the U.P. a separate state would make true what is now false and misleading in some of the Ford Motor Company advertisements. All of the other concerns so partaking can, also, cream from their savings by deletion of the U.P. in their advertising and make similar donations to our cause.

How ludicrous and inane it is that we in the Upper Peninsula continue to be subjugated like shackled, unwanted, bastard children who unfortunately were tacked on to Michigan without political fatherhood. By extortive, political chicanery and reluctant necessity imposed on the Lower Peninsula, we, the inert, and then, hopelessly voiceless, U.P. became a part of Michigan.

...Our future, in separate statehood is as bright as our autumn leaves and as clear as the waters of Lake Superior.

The Ford Motor Company looked into the billboard controversy, discovering that it was the responsibility of an independent automobile dealership. The manager of their corporate advertising department wrote back to Ted, telling him at the end of the letter, "Please be assured that Ford Motor Company does indeed recognize the importance and contributions of Michigan's splendid Upper Peninsula. We do not and will not ever disparage that important region in any of our advertising." No checks were enclosed in the letter.

Ted studied the atlases and discovered that the State of Superior would be 42nd in size and 49th in population in the United States. Statehood supporters devised a secret hand greeting, holding up five fingers on one hand and the index finger on the other.

Reno Perlongo of Watersmeet, a gas station owner, was an enthusiastic advocate of statehood and Ted's efforts. One day as Perlongo stood working at a table saw, he began regaling some high school students with his ideas about the State of Superior. Losing his concentration, he ran his hand through the saw, cutting off his thumb!

Ted told the *Pick & Axe* that Perlongo had earned himself the first Purple Heart in defense of Superior. A few weeks later the veteran found himself standing in front of NBC news cameras, his left hand hanging in a sling over his stomach as he was interviewed about the 51st State of Superior movement.

In 1975 the *Chicago Tribune* carried a long article about the U.P. statehood movement. Ted told them that "It's farther from Ironwood to Detroit than it is from Detroit to New York City." The article pointed out that "in years to come... signs might point to the Albert Building on Suffolk Street where the 'Father of the 51st State,' Ted Albert, conceived his vision of self-government for the 'long suffering' Upper Peninsula of Michigan."

```
_____ 19_____
THE U.P. 51st STATE OF SUPERIOR, INC.
       OFFICIAL MEMBERSHIP CARD
This is to certify that
_____
has paid dues for the year indicated hereon
in_____Chapter, No._____
located at_____, Michigan.

_____
        Financial Secretary
```
(Not Valid Unless Countersigned — Member's Signature)

The publicity created a lot of interest from people in and outside of the U.P. Some writers did not like the name Superior and suggested others. In April 1975 a woman from Chicago wrote to him suggesting that the new state be named 'Algonquin' or 'Winnebago.' A man from the U.P. with eccentric writing habits sent Ted a four-page letter two years later, pointing out that the name Superior reminded people of the cold shores of Lake Superior, and that the name 'Marylord' would be "very pleasing to God."

All of the publicity about his 51st state movement prompted Ted to tell one reporter, "Suddenly the Upper Peninsula has been discovered by the same people who used to ask me if I lived in a teepee." It is true that Ted resembled an American Indian with his dark Middle Eastern complexion.

He told everybody that he was the "governor-designate" of the new state, which he expected to come into being by the beginning of the 1980s. Ted felt that "even if we don't get a new state, we are already getting a new state of affairs." He told another newspaper, "Rest stops in the Lower Peninsula have heated restrooms with piped in music for the happy truck drivers. You get up here and you get outhouses."

Sometime around 1976, just in time for the United States Bicentennial, Ted had a twenty-pound iron bell made at the Motor Casting Company in Milwaukee. The little bell was encircled around its base with the inscription, THE U. P. 51ST STATE OF SUPERIOR, SUUM CUIQUE TRIBUERE [To render to everyone his own]." He proudly posed with the bell in at least two newspaper articles, and even had a State of Superior flag made which featured the bell as the primary element of its design. The bell was to have been rung at Marquette, the provisional capital; Ted prepared sheets of paper entitled "The 51st State Bell Ringers," with lines for people to write down their names and addresses.

During the Bicentennial year Ted told a newspaper, "Our colonial pioneers, with less numbers and against a more formidable adversary, proceeded undaunted by the flailing tongue or the enormity of their project. They sought a new freedom and independence and obtained it. So it will be—for the U.P."

He said he had "spent over $3,000 for stationery, posters, arm bands, and stuff like that... Some newspapers say I made my footnote in history, and that I should shut up, but I find this a new opportunity to hit upon statehood for the U.P."

Ted's friend and supporter Mike Cowdery produced nearly 10,000 window and 4,000 bumper stickers promoting the State of Superior, along with a ten-foot long banner. He figured he had close to $3,500 invested in State of Superior material. Ted himself ordered membership cards for the U. P. 51st State of Superior, Inc., as well as letterheads and envelopes, and various posters and advertising bills. Besides that, there were also buttons, license plates and clothing as others jumped aboard the promotion bandwagon.

The buttons were 2-1/4 inches in diameter and carried a Biblical quotation from Matthew, Chapter 19, verse 30: "And the last shall be first," an allusion to the fact that even though the U.P. might become the "last" or 51st state, it would still, in Ted's opinion, be the "first."

The last great push for statehood took place in 1977, with meetings held at the Mather Inn in Ishpeming in May, and in Marquette the following month. Ted's greatest challenge was to carry out research and file a lawsuit in the federal courts. He was convinced that he could file such a suit in either Marquette or Grand Rapids, and it was being contemplated in 1976 and 1977.

Ted told supporters that the Ojibwas did not give up the U.P. to the federal government until several years after it was given to Lower Michigan in 1837. He told them that "if my suit is successful, the Upper Peninsula will revert to territorial status. We will then take steps to have Congress admit the Upper Peninsula into the Union as the 51st state."

His suit would request a declaratory judgment and/or a declaration of rights and liabilities.

One of the most important questions to be asked of the federal court is the question of whether Article 4, Section 3, Part 1 of the United States Constitution is in direct conflict with Amendment 9 of the Bill of Rights.

Article 4 requires the consent of the legislature of Michigan and the consent of Congress as a condition of statehood. Amendment 9 declares inalienable rights are not disparaged even if not found in the Constitution.

The great charters of liberty state that people who bear a real grievance have the right to determine their own destiny.

Ted Albert with his State of Superior Liberty Bell, 1976.

Ted's lawsuit was being anticipated all through May, June and July of 1977, but never materialized. By the beginning of the following year he was too involved in another political campaign to spend much time on the U.P. 51st State of Superior; the movement had reached its zenith in 1976-77, and rapidly faded from the picture in the ensuing years.[15]

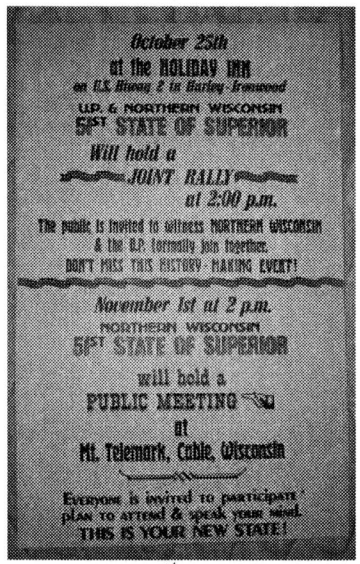

Poster for the 1975 51st State of Superior rallies.

---

[15] Dominic Jacobetti introduced House Bill No. 6115 to the Michigan legislature on March 8, 1978, calling for the adjustment of boundaries between the Upper and Lower Peninsulas, and holding a referendum. The bill was never put to a vote.

10

THE DREAM UNFULFILLED

The separation movement begun by Ted Albert also took root in the northern parts of the Lower Peninsula by the spring of 1979 when a man named Karl Waldner from Boyne City announced himself as the "provisional counselor" of the Independent State of Superior. Waldner requested the Michigan legislature to "allow a vote on separation to be held in the 36 northernmost counties of Michigan." Ted told a reporter, "Everybody's getting into it now. I don't know whether he's a friend, or if he's an upstart and an interloper. I just wonder where some of these people have been for the past five years since we formally filed as a corporate structure that is duly qualified to be the legal vehicle for the formation of the State of Superior."

Despite this momentary spotlight on statehood, the idea was soon all but forgotten, except by Ted and a few loyal supporters. In December of 1979 he announced another run for the United States Congress; "I believe there are a lot of people who will vote for me so I can introduce the enabling act to initiate separate statehood for the Upper Peninsula.... I am not a one issue candidate..."

During his campaign he told a group called the "Concerned Christian Women,"

I have a track record of living by the 10 Commandments.

I call upon the Holy Father every day to help me banish from our society, hate, poverty, hunger, thirst, and pain so that all men may live together in the harmony He meant for us to.

I beseech in silent prayer that He look on my shoulders and guide me in the ways that I should act.

I am an attorney that has spent his career protecting the poor, the aggrieved, the injured and the demeaned in our society to the extent that I am pure but yet pure and wholesome of mind and body. My record is replete with my good deeds.

Ted and Superior　　　　　***By Bruce K. Cox***

Ted was then living in Iron River, and was introduced to a crowd at the Happy Italian restaurant on June 17, 1980, as "a fighter, a man of integrity, a people's lawyer who will fight not for power and money, but for the interests of the people and for what is right." Ten days later the Iron County Democrats gave him their unanimous endorsement, following which he read them one of his favorite poems, of his own composition:

>I'm ready to serve as I conceive,
>To express my thoughts—and what
>>I believe.
>
>I pat no one—I cast no slurs,
>But fight for what is mine—
>>and your's.
>
>I claim no super clarity,

> Just a sense of justice—and
>   sincerity.
> I'm not too old—I'm not too
>   young.
> But clear of mind—and fluid
>   tongue.
> Can't reach me with a 10 foot
>   pole.
> Friends are many and I'm all
>   whole.
> Poor of pocket—rich of mind,
> No fruits of money—so unkind.
> If you're for me—I hope you are,
> You've hitched your wagon to a star!

Ted attended his 45th class reunion in July, serving as master of ceremonies. When the primary election took place in August 1980, Ted made a good showing, but still came in third with 11,000 votes; the winner was Dan Dorrity with 14,500, with Herb Stephens coming in second with 11,300. He mustered up enough energy to run in another race in 1982, losing again in the primary, this time to Kent Bourland.

But this was not the last of Ted Albert on the U.P. political scene. In 1984 he made his final bid for office, once again running for Congress, unsuccessfully facing off against four democratic opponents. He was still actively involved in his law practice, and the State Bar was still carrying on investigations into claims of disgruntled clients, but nothing comparable to what took place in the 1970s.

Ted's dream of securing statehood for the U.P., like his dream of being elected to public office, was never to be realized. His health began to decline in the mid-80s as he suffered from the ravages of diabetes, and he passed away on the afternoon of February 5, 1989 at the Iron County Medical Care Facility in Crystal Falls at age seventy-one, following a stroke. A memorial service was held at St. Agnes Catholic

Church in Iron River, and the next spring his ashes were interred at Riverside Cemetery in Ironwood.

Thus ended the long and colorful career of a man who stands out as an unheralded giant in the history of the Gogebic Iron Range and the Upper Peninsula of Michigan. He strove for something big and out of the ordinary. What he tried to do required independent thinking, an ability to see beyond the shackles which time and circumstances had forged around the U.P., self-assurance, and a fearless disregard for the naysayers and detractors. Should the U. P. statehood movement ever rise again and reach fruition, Ted Albert may indeed go down in history as the "Father of the 51st State."

Notes on Sources

1 The Middle East Meets the U.P.

Information on George Albert comes from his obituary, a short bio and news published in the *Ironwood Daily Globe*, from immigration records available online at Ellis Island website, the 1920 U. S. Census, his marriage record, Gogebic Range directories, Gogebic County court records, and from a website about the Koura region of Lebanon. Also the obituaries of his wife, children, and brothers; real estate records at the Gogebic County Courthouse, and the printed record of his lawsuit against Gamble-Skogmo, Inc., Cal. No. 45385, appealed to the Michigan Supreme Court. Anecdote about the hookah was provided by Joe Carlson, a former neighbor.

2 Birth of a Legal Career

Ted Albert's early life is reconstructed from his obituary and other articles appearing in the *Ironwood Daily Globe*, from Gogebic County Court File No. 71-5, from autobiographical details he compiled and submitted to the Michigan State Library and used in his political campaigns, and from records of the Northland Sports Club and Gogebic County court records.

3 Prosecuting Attorney

Ted's career as Gogebic County Prosecuting Attorney is documented in articles from the *Ironwood Daily Globe*, in Gogebic County Court File No. 71-5 and other court records, opinions of the Michigan State Attorney General, and from material he used in his political campaigns. For the hospital controversy, see "A Statement of Public Interest, November 23, 1962," and the *Bessemer Herald*.

4 Democratic Dissenters

Most of the history of The State Democratic Club of Michigan comes from posters, letters and brochures printed by the Club, from newspaper reports appearing in the *Detroit Free Press, Detroit News, Detroit Times, Ironwood Daily Globe, Marquette Mining*

Journal, *Detroit Southwest Journal*, *Escanaba Daily Press*, *Iron Mountain News*, *Grand Rapids Press*, and *Grand Rapids Herald*, and the Club's incorporation record. Background on Frank Hook can be found in his daughter Mary Hook Allen's book, *Fightin' Frank, The Biography of Upper Peninsula's 12th District Democratic Congressman*, and in Ted's campaign materials.

5 Trials

Ted composed a letter concerning the 1959 Steelworkers strike and the implications of the Taft-Hartley Act. His mock bill of complaint for divorce of the U. P. from Lower Michigan is partially quoted in "Michigan's Superior Notion," by Judith Yates Borger, which appeared in the Sept.-Oct. 1977 issue of *Northliner Magazine*. His career during this period is partially reconstructed from Gogebic County Court File No. 71-5, from the printed transcript of Case No. 13,919 in U. S. Court of Appeals for the 6th District, Norman Zachary and Edward Zacharski vs. U.S.A.; from their petition for Writ of Certiorari to the U. S. Court of Appeals for the 6th Circuit, in the Supreme Court of the U.S., 1959; reports in the *Ironwood Daily Globe* and *Milwaukee Sentinel*; U.S. Court of Appeals, U. S. A. vs. Peter E. Bradt and Theodore G. Albert, on the internet at cases.justia.com, Case 294 F.2d 879 for background on the contempt charges; *Marquette Mining Journal*, "Upper Peninsula Independence Movement Renewed...," March 9, 1962; Ted's handwritten 'declaration of independence' of the U.P. from 1962; autobiographical material he provided to the State Library of Michigan; the printed transcript, "Brief of Theodore G. Albert On Appeal" for Cases No. 52,580, 52,581 and 52,582 concerning contempt charges in the Pitts, Dogan and Fittante cases; Peter Lazaros information is found at cases.justia.com, Case 480 F.2d 174 U. S. A. vs. Peter N. Lazaros; a *Time Magazine* website reproducing an article dated May 15, 1978; and an undated newspaper clipping from the *Detroit Free Press*, "Lazaros' Pal Faces Disbarment," about attorney James H. Hudnut; also an article from the *Ironwood Daily Globe*, June 16, 1969, "Says Mafia Informer Lying;" *Detroit News* article about Daniel Zahari, whose wife filed a grievance against Ted many years later.

6 Tribulations

This part of Ted's life is documented by a reminiscence provided by a former legal secretary, and an anecdote from a local lawyer; by Ted's campaign materials, by reports in the *Ironwood Daily Globe*, and by Gogebic County Court Files No. 70-16 and 71-5; various records of the Michigan State Bar Grievance Board case, including U. S. Court of Appeals for the 6th Circuit, No. 75-1163, Theodore G. Albert vs. The State Bar of Michigan, et al; State of Michigan in the Supreme Court, Case No. 54221, State Bar File No. 28670-1; State of Michigan in the Supreme Court, Appeal from State Bar Grievance Court (same case numbers as previous): Brief and Appendix of Respondent, and Brief and Appendix of State Bar; U. S. District Court for the Western District of Michigan, File No. 74-99 CA; reports in the *Bessemer Pick & Axe*, *Duluth News Tribune*, and *Nonesuch News*; his case for reinstatement decided by the Michigan Supreme Court is found on the internet at adbmich.org, "In the Matter of the Reinstatement of Theodore G. Albert, No. 34422-A."

7 The Candidate

Ted's political career is documented by numerous pieces of campaign literature and materials, by reports and ads appearing in the *Ironwood Daily Globe*, *Bessemer Pick & Axe*, *Iron County Miner* (Hurley, Wis.), and *Duluth News Tribune*; by press releases, articles prepared for publication in the *Houghton Daily Mining Gazette*; his service as attorney for a defendant in the "Deep Throat" case, appealed to the U. S. Court of Appeals for the 6th District can be found on the internet. His participation in Project LEAD in Lansing is documented by a thank-you letter sent to him. Frank Hook's attempt to aid him in his campaign is documented by a copy of Hood's letter to Andrew J. Biemiller in 1978.

8 The Politics of Yooper Separatism

Reminiscence of a former legal secretary; *Latifundia in Gitche Gumee*, by Benjamin F. Smith. Also an article entitled, "Ahonen Against Government Land Acquisition Program," in the

Ironwood Daily Globe, Oct. 11, 1967; *The U.P. Landowner*; *Bessemer Pick & Axe*; resolution adopted by the U.P. 51st State of Superior; *Northliner Magazine*, Sept-Oct 1977; reports in the *Ironwood Daily Globe*; *The Superior Idea*, Vol. 1, No. 1, Sept. 24, 1975, for resolution of the Vilas Co., Wis. board; *The Upper Peninsula Observer*, a campaign newspaper published in August 1978 for the Pat Kitzman campaign; "Creed Of The Citizens Committee For Better Government, Inc.," dated Jan. 4, 1978; political questionnaires from various groups/organizations, answered by Ted Albert.

9 Fighting for Superior

Most of Ted's statehood efforts were chronicled in newspaper articles in the mid to late-1970s, and included articles from the *Ironwood Daily Globe, Bessemer Pick & Axe, Marquette Mining Journal, Duluth News Tribune, Sault Ste. Marie Evening News, Iron Mountain News, Chicago Tribune, The Superior Idea,* and *Northliner Magazine*; also U.P. 51st State of Superior literature and posters.

10 The Dream Unfulfilled

Ted's response to Karl Waldner's effort appeared in the *Bessemer Pick & Axe*. His political career is documented by his press releases and campaign literature, and responses to questionnaires; the campaigns were reported on in the *Ironwood Daily Globe* and the *Bessemer Pick & Axe*; obituary and death certificate.

INDEX

A

A & C Promotions, 57
A & P Store, 10, 11
A. D. Johnston High School, 17
Abdallah family, 1
Abdallah, Abadallah, 1
Abdallah, Georges, 2
Abdallah, Habib, 2
Abdallah, Martha, 2
Abraham, Jacob, 4
Ahonen, Roy, 79
Alaska Statehood Committee, 91
Albert Building, 14, 76, 94
Albert Store, 6, 17
Albert, Dorothy Beauchamp, nee Sobotta, 49, 81
Albert, George, (grandfather of Ted), 1
Albert, George, (father of Ted), 2-15, 56
Albert, Dr. James, 27
Albert, John, (uncle of Ted), 1, 2
Albert, John, (brother of Ted), 14
Albert, Lulu,
  nee Hydar, 5, 9, 12-15
Albert, Marie, nee Mollrud, 16
Albert, Mose, 1, 2, 8
Albert, Sam, (uncle of Ted), 1, 2
Albert, Dr. Samuel, (brother of Ted), 20-22, 27, 28, 41
Albert, Theodore G. "Ted,"
  a tenacious lawyer, and promoter of separate statehood, 1
  his family background, 1-14
  his birth, and school days, 15
  college education, 15
  first marriage, 16
  service in WW2, 16
  sports promotion, 16-18, 26
  passes bar exam, 17
  begins legal practice, 17
  runs for prosecuting atty., 18
  career as Gogebic County Pros. Atty., 19-29
  memberships, 19, 20

Albert, Theodore G. "Ted," cont'd,
  battle with Grand View Hospital Board, 20-22, 27-29, 41
  inquest into Penokee mine disaster, 22-25
  establishes powers of elected officials, 25
  Sunday Lake mine strike, 25
  bingo game controversy, 26
  runs for circuit judge (1953), 26
  active in democratic party, 30
  first run (1956) for Congress, 30, 31
  friendship with Frank Hook, 31, 32, 68, 71
  disgruntled with Gov. Williams, 32
  forms State Democratic Club, 33
  runs for prosecuting atty. in 1958 primary, 39
  opinions on Taft-Hartley Act, 40
  mock bill of complaint for divorce of U.P. from lower Mich., 41
  charged with contempt of court, 43
  candidate for delegate to Mich. Constitutional Convention, 43-45
  writes declaration of U.P. independence, 45-46
  maintains office at Stambaugh, 46
  submits bio to state library, 46, 47
  second run (1964) for Congress, 47
  association with Wisok, 33, 47
  association with Goldfarb & Hudnut, 47-49
  the Fittante case, 48, 49
  second marriage, 49
  partnerhip with Peter Barbara, 49
  the Lazaros case, 49-50
  acquaintance with Daniel Zahari, 50
  enthusiasm for righting wrongs, 51
  problems with State Bar, 51, 53, 54, 56-62
  runs for district judge (1970), 52

INDEX

Albert, Theodore G. "Ted," cont'd,
  suit against *Ironwood Daily Globe*, 54-56
  family lawsuit, 56
  fourth run (1978) for Congress, 61, 69-74
  cleared by supreme court, 62-64
  third run (1974) for Congress, 64
  involvement in Human Rights Party, 64-70, 91
  the *Deep Throat* case, 64
  runs for U.S. senate, 68-69
  opposition to Project Elf / Seafarer / Sanguine, 65, 72, 80, 81
  conflict with Jacobetti, 81, 82
  connection with Joe Mack, 83
  addresses Vilas County Board, 84
  supports separate statehood movement in northern Wis., 84, 85
  opinion of Jimmy Carter, 88
  begins U.P. 51st State of Superior movement, 91
  riled by Ford billboard, 92, 93
  called "Father of 51st State," 94
  orders a 51st State bell, 95, 97
  plans a lawsuit to separate U.P. from lower Mich., 95, 96
  fifth run (1980) for Congress, 99-101
  sixth run (1982) for Congress, 101
  seventh run (1984) for Congress, 101
  his health declines, 101
  his death at Crystal Falls, 101
  his legacy, 102
Allen, Mary, nee Hook, 31
Alsco Aluminum, 47
American News Distributing Co., 64
American News Co., Inc., 64
Americans for Democratic Action, 35
anti-Sanguine resolution, 81
AuTrain, Mich., 72

B

Baird, William S., atty., 51
ball clubs, 17
Barbara, Peter, atty., 49
Barkley, Alben, Truman's v. p., 31
Barr, Henry, 9, 10
Beirut, Lebanon, 2
Bessemer, Mich., 17, 20, 45, 60, 66, 80, 91
Bolognesi, William, 30
Boulogne, France, 2
Bourland, Kent, 101
Bove, Armand, atty., 58
Boyne City, Mich., 99
Bradt, Peter, 41-43
Brandner, Phillip A., 84
Brunetta, Arthur, 84
Buck, Curtis, atty., 6
Burns, Robert A., 22

C

Calumet, Mich., 33
Carter, Jimmy, U.S. President, 81, 88
Chicago, Ill., 94
Chicago and Northwestern Railroad, 3
Cifelli, Gus, atty., 57, 62
CIO, 32, 34, 51, 69
Cirilli, Armand, 73
Citizen's Committee for Better Government Inc., 73, 88
Clark, Charles M., 4, 5
Clarkson, S. James, 49
Cleveland, Ohio, 6
Clevenger, Raymond, 47
Club Chicaugon, 57
Committee to Elect Theodore G. Albert To Congress, 88
Committee To Elect Theodore G. Albert U. S. Senator, 68
Concerned Christian Women, 99
Cowdery, Mike, 60, 66, 80, 95

INDEX

Creed of The Citizen's Committee, 88
Croker, Robert L., Sr., 84

D

Daily Mining Gazette, 71
Davis & Fehr Department Store, 8
Davis, Bob, U.S. senator, 82
Davis, "Boo Boo," 50
Dawson, William, 11
Dearborn, Mich., 50
Deep Throat pornography case, 64
Delaney, Roy, atty., 58
Democratic Central Committee, 32, 34
Department of Natural Resources, 19, 65, 80
Detroit News, 36, 38, 50
Detroit, Mich., 16, 32-34, 36-39, 41, 44, 47, 49, 50, 59, 81, 91, 94
Diggs, Charles M., 34
divorce of Upper Peninsula from Lower Michigan, 41, 91
Dogans case, 48, 51
Dorrity, Dan, 101
Drazkowski, Frank, 27
Duluth News Tribune, 61, 70, 71
Durand, Mich., billboard controversy, 92
Dussault, Francis, 84

E

Eagle River, Wis., 85
Edwards, George, 36
Egizi, Rudy, 15
Everson, Hans, 7, 9, 11

F

Father of the 51st State, 94
Federal Reserve System, 72
Fehr, Fred, 8
Fehr, Maud W., 8
Ferency, Zolton, 65
Fih-El-Koura, Lebanon, 3, 5
Fisher Fleetwood, 16
Fisher Body Division, General Motors Corp., 16
Fittante case, 48, 49
Foley, David, policeman, 4
Ford Motor Co., 33, 92, 93
Forster, Thomas, 85

G

Gamble-Skogmo, 11, 12
gambling, 45, 58, 85
Gaylord, Mich., 82
George, James, 13
Gerovac, George, 75
Glaeser, John, 84
Gogebic Community College, 15
Gogebic County, 1, 11, 12, 15, 19, 20, 22, 25, 27, 66
Gogebic County Prosecuting Attorney, 1, 17-20, 22, 25, 26, 59
Gogebic Ministerial Assn., 17
Gogebic Iron Range, 40, 102
Goldfarb and Hudnut, 47-49
Grand Rapids, Mich., 37, 96
Grand View Hospital, 20-2, 27, 29, 41, 61
Great Atlantic and Pacific Tea Co., 10
Grendatti, Anthony, 33
Grit magazine, 91

H

Haj, Mrs. S., 1
Hamati, Rev. Elias, 5
Hamm Brewing Co., 17
Hardy, Raymond, 88
Hart, Philip, Michigan senator, 34, 37
Hellman, Rusty, state rep., 86
Holiday Inn, 51st State of Superior rally, 85

INDEX

Hook, Frank E., U.S. Congressman, 20, 30-36, 39, 69, 72
Houghton, Mich., 71, 81
Hubbard, Orville, 50
Hudnut, James, atty., 49
Humphrey, Charles, Sr., atty., 8
Humphrey, Charles M, Jr., atty., 55
Hurley, Wis., 73, 85
Hydar, Karem, or Karemia, 1

I

Independent State of Superior, 99
Iron Mountain, Mich., 3, 4, 33
Iron River, Mich., 53, 57, 100, 102
Ironwood Daily Globe, 17, 21, 26, 37, 45, 53-56, 58, 59, 91
Ironwood, Mich., 2, 3, 5, 7, 8, 13-17, 19, 22, 24, 31-33, 37, 41, 47, 49, 53, 54, 58, 59, 62, 67, 73, 79, 83, 91, 94, 102
Ishpeming, Mich., 79, 96

J

Jacobetti, Dominic, state rep., 81-83, 98
Jacquart, Lionel, 11
Jamrich, John, 86
Jetty, Jack, 33
John family, 5
Johnson, Peter, justice of the peace, 4
Johnson, William L., 32-34, 36, 44, 45

K

Kavanagh, Thomas, Michigan Supreme Court Justice, 54
Kelley, Frank, Mich. Atty Gen., 83
Kent, W. Wallace, Dist. Judge, 41-43
Khoury, Mr., 5, 7

Khoury, Sam, 4
Kitzman, Pat, 81, 86-88
Kiwani's Key Club, 15
Klassen, Ray, 84
Koura District, Lebanon, 1
Kramer, Richard, 56

L

L'Anse, Mich., 31
Laggis, George, 10
Laggis, Nick, 10
Laine, Reino, 24
Laitala, Matt, 65, 80, 86
Lake Michigan, 72
Lake Superior, 72, 93, 94
Landers, Thomas J., Circuit Judge, 26, 61
Lansing, Mich., 33, 45, 48, 56, 57, 64, 65, 83, 91
Larson, Bernard, Prosecuting Atty., 17, 18
Latifundia in Gitchee Gumee, 77
Lauerman Brothers Co., 5
Lazaros, Peter, 49, 50
Lebanon, Lebanese, 1-3, 5, 7, 14
Lesinski, John, state rep., 33
Lesinksi, Mr., judge, 50
Lieberthal, Dr. Paul, 10, 11
Little Bay De Noc, Mich., 72
Luther L. Wright H. S. 15, 17

M

Mack, Joseph, 30, 31, 83
Mafia, 49
Magnuson, Karl, 79, 80
Maki, William, 8
Manistique, Mich., 72
Marenisco, Mich., 75
Marquette Mining Journal, 86, 91
Marquette, Mich., 41, 42, 73, 95, 96
Martin, Homer, 32-34, 37, 38
Martinac, Peter, 33
Mass City, Mich., 71-73, 88
Massie, Edward, 10

INDEX

Matchwood Twp., Mich., 79, 80, 86
Mather Inn, 96
McBrearty, William J., 58
McKernan, Edward J., 16
McLeod, Keith, 73, 75
Michigan Constitutional
  Convention, 43
Michigan Human Rights Party, 64, 68, 70, 91
Michigan State Bar, 17, 19, 58, 73, 101
Michigan State Bar Grievance
  Board, 1, 48, 49, 51, 56-62
Michigan State Democratic
  Central Committee, 32, 34
Michigan Supreme Court, 13, 22, 48, 49, 53, 54, 58-62, 73
Michigan Technological
  University, 81
Milliken, William, Gov. of
  Mich., 60, 63
Mills, C. Wright, 80
Milwaukee, Wis., 95
"Mr. X" case, 57, 58
Model Clothing Store, 8
Mohardt, Michael T., 32-34, 37, 38
Montgomery Ward, 11
Moose Lodge, 20
Morton House, 38
Motor Casting Co., 95
Munising, Mich., 72

N

Nadolney, Jerome, 39
National Right To Work
  Committee, 73
Negaunee, Mich., 81
New York City, 2, 94
Newport, Ky., 64
Nicholas family, 5
Nickeles, Carem, 1
Nonesuch News, 62
Norrie mine, 22
Northern Michigan University, 73, 86
Northern Wisconsin 51st State of
Superior, Inc., 85
Northland Sports Club, 17, 26
Northland Sports Organization, 16
Nyman, Theodore, mine
  inspector, 24, 25

O

O'Konski, Alvin, Wis.
  congressman, 85
Office of Price Administration, 17
Ontonagon County, 52, 53, 79
Operation Action U. P., 80
Orthodox Christians, 3, 5, 13
Ottawa National Forest, 78-79

P

Pabst mine, 22
Panama Canal Zone giveaway, 88
Patek, Julius J., 4, 5, 15
Patek, Solomon W., 15
Pellow, William, 39, 45
Penobscot Building, 41, 49, 57
Penokee Ore Co., 22-5
Penttila, John, 44
Perlich, Frank, 45
Perlongo, Reno, 93
Peterson, Melvin D., 88
Pick & Axe, 60, 66, 74, 75, 80, 81, 91, 93
Piggly Wiggly Store, 11
Pitts case, 48, 51
pornography panel, 64
Presque Isle, Wis., 85
S. S. Pretoria, 2
Project Elf, 72
Project Sanguine, 72, 80, 81
Project Seafarer, 65, 72, 80

R

Redford Twp., Mich., 56
Reuther, Walter, 32, 35, 36, 39
Riegelhaupt, Isadore, 6

INDEX

Riegelhaupt, J. M., 6
Romney, George, Gov. of Mich., 39
Rosenzweig, Louis, 56
Roth, Stephen, Mich. Atty. Gen., 21
Rothbard, Murray N., 72
Rowell, Ralph, state rep., 24
Rulle, Jack, 18

S

Saginaw, Mich., 56
Sault Ste. Marie, Mich., 45, 47
Schmidt, Laird Brooks, 85
Scholle, Gus, 32, 35, 36
Seaman Bros., 10
secret hand greeting, 93
Senter, Richard, 56, 61
Shea, Jerry F., 8
Shea, John, 7, 8
Simon, Mrs. George, 1
Sims, Albert, 18
Smith, Benjamin F., 77-78
Smith, Raymond, 81
Soo locks, 72
St. Simon church, 2, 5, 13
St. Ignace, Mich., 45
Staebler, Neil, 31, 32, 34, 36
Stambaugh, Mich., 46, 49
State Democratic Club of Michigan, 33, 34, 36-39, 44
State of Algonquin, 94
State of Hiawatha, 78
State of Marylord, 94
State of Superior, 14, 41, 46, 51, 65, 67, 70, 71, 77, 80, 83, 85, 89, 91-99
State of Winnebago, 94
Steelworkers Union, 22, 25, 36, 40
Stephens, Herb, 101
Sunday Lake mine, 25
Superior Steel Fabricating Co., 83
Superior 51st State tee shirts, 83
Superior Border Patrol armbands, 91
Swainson, John B., 37, 59
Sylvania, 79

T

Taft-Hartley Act, 40
The Prime Principle, 77
The U. P. Landowner, 79
Topaz, Mich., 79
Trethewey, Clifford, 26
Tripoli, Lebanon, 1
Truman, Harry, U.S. President, 31
Tryon, Elmer, 54, 55, 59

U

U. P. trade deficit, 73
U. P. 51st State of Superior, Inc., the, 14, 67, 76, 80, 81, 84, 86, 91, 95, 98
U. P. 51st State Bell Ringers, 95
U. S. Forest Service, 78-79
Union for Democratic Action, 35
United States Steel Corp., 33
United States Supreme Court, 53
University of Wisconsin, 15
Upper Peninsula Federation of Land Owners, 79
Upper Peninsula colleges, 86
Upper Peninsula tax revenues, 85-86
Upper Peninsula Declaration of Independence, 45, 46

V

Vandenberg, Arthur H., Senator, 32
Van Wagoner, Murray, Gov. of Mich., 33
Vilas County, Wis., 83-84
voter initiatives, 72

W

Wakefield, Mich., 25, 31
Waldner, Karl, 99
Wall Street Journal, 39
Walleye Street Journal, 85

INDEX

Waples and Waples, attys., 10
Waples, Belmont, atty., 7
War Production Board, 16
Warren, Mich., 56
Washington, D. C., 35
Watersmeet, Mich., 19, 92
Weis, Lawrence, atty., 55
Western Upper Peninsula Planning and Development Region aka WUPPDR, 80
White Pine, Mich., 62
Wilkes-Barre, Penn., 3
Williams, G. Mennen, Gov. of Mich., 19, 24, 32, 33, 35-37, 39, 59, 73
Willys-Overland Co., 10
Winona, Minn., 16
Wisco Aluminum, 47
Wisok, Norton N., 33, 38, 39, 41
Wisok, Robert, 41, 47
WNMU TV, 73
Wylie, Robert, 45

Y

Yanney, Rev. Nicola 5
Yooper[s] 72, 77, 86, 89, 92
Ypsilanti, Mich. 31

Z

Zahari, Daniel, 50
Zimpelmann, E. C., 84
Zinn, Eugene, Dist. Judge, 52, 54, 59